Life Principles for
THE STORMS OF LIFE

Life Principles for
THE STORMS OF LIFE

SHERRY CARTER

Advancing the Ministries of the Gospel
AMG Publishers

God's Word to you is our highest calling.

Following God

LIFE PRINCIPLES FROM THE STORMS OF LIFE

Published by AMG Publishers. All Rights Reserved.

First Printing, 2010

ISBN 13: 978-0-89957-028-0
ISBN 10: 0-89957-028-3

Edited by Rich Cairnes and Rick Steele
Interior layout by Jennifer Ross and Rick Steele

Cover design by Taylor Ware at Indoor Graphics Corporation, Chattanooga, TN
http://www.indoorgraphics.com/

Printed in Canada
15 14 13 12 11 10 –T– 6 5 4 3 2 1

Other new releases in the Following God® Series:

Life Principles from Paul's Co-Workers
by Richard Soule

and

**Life Principles for Worship
from the Feasts of Israel**
by Rick Shepherd

Look for these new Following God® study books in
your local Christian book stores or on our websites:
www.AMGPublishers.com
www.FollowingGod.com

Acknowledgments

This journey has been exciting and overwhelming. Many times I gave up, certain that I couldn't complete the task God had given me. A dear circle of friends prayed for me and encouraged me. Pat, Leah, Cindy, and Margaret, this study wouldn't exist without you.

I owe a special debt of gratitude to Karen Johnson. She read and re-read each page. She checked every punctuation mark and verified every Scripture reference. She challenged me and often stretched my patience. My work and my life are both enriched by her friendship and faithfulness.

There are many others who supported me through this project. The ladies who attended my "test" classes endured my teaching and my questions about the organization of the chapters and the clarity of the wording. Their willingness to be honest was invaluable. The members of Cedar Bayou Baptist Church, Baytown, Texas—especially the Chronological Sunday School Class—encouraged me and lifted me up in prayer.

Above all, I must thank my husband, Charles. He endured much as I worked on this. He often kept the house running and he ate a lot of fast food. Perhaps he, more than anyone else, rejoices to see this work completed.

I present this to You, Jesus. I long to see You. I adore You more than anyone or anything on this Earth.

 SHERRY CARTER

About the Author

Sherry Carter's first Bible Study manuscript, *Storms of Life*, won the 2007 Award of Excellence at the Blue Ridge Mountain Christian Writer's Conference and became the basis for this Following God® workbook study. As part of a military family, Sherry experienced first-hand several world cultures. She began her career at M.D. Anderson Cancer Hospital and later became an engineer at Johnson Space Center in Houston, Texas. During Sherry's last few years at JSC, she experienced a series of agonizing crises, including the loss of the space shuttle Columbia and its crew and the deaths of her mother and father-in-law. After being laid off from JSC in 2006, God led her to write *Storms of Faith*, allowing her to share the lessons He taught her as He brought her through anger and confusion to a deeper faith in Him. Sherry combines this life experience with thirty years as a Bible study teacher to bring depth to her writing. She lives in Baytown, Texas, with her husband and an adopted greyhound.

About the Following God Series

Three authors and fellow ministers, Wayne Barber, Eddie Rasnake, and Rick Shepherd, teamed up in 1998 to write a character-based Bible study for AMG Publishers. Their collaboration developed into the title, *Life Principles from the Old Testament.* Since 1998, these same authors and AMG Publishers have produced four more character-based studies—each consisting of twelve lessons geared around a five-day study of a particular Bible personality. More studies of this type are in the works. New authors have recently been acquired, and new types of studies have been published in an ongoing effort to add fresh perspectives as to what it means to follow God. However, the interactive study format that readers have come to love remains constant in all of our newest titles. As new Bible studies are being planned, our focus remains the same: to provide excellent Bible study materials that point people to God's Word in ways that allow them to apply truths to their own lives. More information on this groundbreaking series along with a free leader's guide for this study can be found on the following web page:

www.amgpublishers.com

Preface

Life Principles for the Storms of Life grew out of a time of great trial and suffering in my life. During this time my faith was shaken, then rocked to the core, and finally devastated. My Jesus, in His love and tenderness, never left me; He held me in His arms each step of the way. He mended my shattered faith and prayed for me when I had no words of my own. He comforted me, strengthened me, and gave me the peace that passes all understanding (Philippians 4:7). He gave me victory even when the world around me expected me to be destroyed forever.

Even now, He continues to lead me to His Word, teaching me His purposes for my journey. I'm praying for you as you begin this study, that He will reveal His purpose for your journey. No matter your circumstances, God is with you. He sustains you and is sufficient to meet all your needs. He will strengthen your faith, guide you with His Word, and bring you victory.

As the sky darkens with suffering, His truth will strengthen you. As the storm intensifies, His presence will carry you. When the storm has passed, His love will bring peace and healing to your heart.

Whether you are studying *Life Principles for the Storms of Life* alone or in a group, allow the Holy Spirit to guide you. He will reveal God's truth to you and teach you to apply it to your life.

Praise God for the storm!

SHERRY

Table of Contents

1

Focus on Faith

We live in a time of crisis. Daily headlines speak of earthquakes, floods, and famine. The nightly news is filled with stories of crime in every neighborhood, explanations of the latest economic issue threatening financial security, and descriptions of a new disease that hovers on the edge of an epidemic. As believers, we pray to our Almighty Sovereign Lord to deliver those who suffer and to protect our loved ones. Our faith can become tattered and worn as we hear of the things happening in nations all around the world, in urban and rural areas . We look at each other and ask, "What is our world coming to? Is God still in control? How can He allow these terrible things to happen day after day?"

It's even more overwhelming as we listen to our friends, church family, and co-workers. There are trials and difficulties everywhere we look. Good people dealing with illness, difficult family issues, seemingly hopeless financial situations—our prayer list seems to go on and on. Our faith can be weakened as we pray continuously for these people and yet we watch their suffering continue. Is God so busy with the disasters and wars sweeping the world that He has no time to care for His children?

As you study this week, I pray you'll see that God is indeed with you and that He cares for you beyond words. He sustains your faith through His Word and His promises. He allows you to learn of His character and teaches you deeper truths as He carries you through the storm.

Faith is the expression of our confidence in God, in His promises, and His work in our lives.

"He [God] alone is my rock and my salvation; he is my fortress, I will never be shaken."

Psalms 62:2

FAITH IS ...

For many of us, faith is difficult to define. Is it a feeling? Is it a conscious choice? Is it an elusive quality that only comes with maturity and experience? God's Word teaches us that faith is the expression of our confidence in God, His promises, and His work in our lives.

"Now faith is the substance of things hoped for, the evidence of things not seen." (Hebrews 11:1 NKJV)

Our faith is related to *things hoped for*. This phrase doesn't refer to things we want to happen but aren't sure they will. A better way to say it is "things expected with desire."[1][2] When you await the arrival of a loved one at the airport, you know which flight they're on and you expect to see them— you're filled with great desire for that moment. We must understand that, because the faith of the writer of Hebrews was grounded in Jesus Christ, resurrection and the reward of eternal life were truth. The writer hadn't yet received his eternal reward; he'd not yet been resurrected—but what was reality for Jesus would be reality for him (Philippians 3:10, 11).

Are the words of the Gospel absolute truth for you? Is it reality that Jesus died for your sins? Is your own resurrection expected? In your life, are you nagged by uncertainties, eating away at your security? After reading Psalm 62:2, what does it mean to you to think of your faith as a "substance"?

I love the word substance. There's a solidness to it. Substances have a defined nature and, come what may, they'll always have that defined nature. Carbon has the same chemical structure it had thousands of years ago and it'll have the same chemical structure thousands of years from now. Water is H_2O and it'll be H_2O forever. The word "substance" confirms to me I can be confident in God's Word and, come what may, it will never change. His Word is the bedrock of our faith.

📖 Read the Scripture verses below and put a check by the ones that are "substance" for you.

"The LORD is the everlasting God, the Creator of the ends of the earth. He will not grow tired or weary, and his understanding no one can fathom." (Isaiah 40:28)

"How great is the love the Father has lavished on us, that we should be called the children of God!" (1 John 3:1)

"If we confess our sins, he is faithful and just and will forgive us our sins and purify us from all unrighteousness." (1 John 1:9)

"Surely I am with you always, to the very end of the age." (Matthew 28:20)

"Jesus Christ is the same yesterday and today and forever." (Hebrews 13:8)

"My Father, who has given them to me, is greater than all; no one can snatch them out of my Father's hand." (John 10:29)

"All Scripture is God-breathed and is useful for teaching, rebuking, correcting and training in righteousness." (2 Timothy 3:16)

"And my God will meet all your needs according to his glorious riches in Christ Jesus." (Philippians 4:19)

"The one who is in you is greater than the one who is in the world." (1 John 4:4)

Could you check all the verses above? I admit there've been times in my life when, because of my circumstances, one or two of those truths were in doubt in my mind. There was a time when my suffering overwhelmed me and I was sure God wasn't meeting my deepest needs as promised in Philippians 4:19. I doubted the promise of His presence (Matthew 28:20) and, as the situation worsened, I was afraid Satan was winning the battle. As I cried out to Him, my Father made His presence very real to me and assured me that Satan could never defeat Him (1 John 4:4). I knew He held me in His mighty right hand and would bring ultimate victory to every circumstance.

Pillars of Faith
Even as we struggle through difficult circumstances, two equally important pillars of our faith will confirm God's presence with us: (1) God's Word, with His promises contained within, and (2) our recognition of His work in our daily lives. Let's look at the assurance each can give us.

God's Word and Promises
When we take God's Word into our lives and stand on His promises, the Word becomes a Rock on which our lives are built (Matthew 7:24). His Word brings stability and power into our lives, no matter the circumstances. The enemy, Satan, gains no greater joy than to cripple us by causing us to doubt God's Word.

Remember that Satan is the father of lies and confusion (John 8:44). When you pray for forgiveness, he slinks up to you and tells you that you can't possibly expect God to love you or use you because of a past sin or a present weakness. When you read God's Word, he slithers in, trying to convince you that God's Word is not the truth and not relevant to your world today. When times are hard, he whispers in your ear and tells you God has abandoned you and left you to endure this suffering alone.

When Satan attacks with his lies, we must trust in the truth of God's Word. Call out to the Holy Spirit for guidance and clarity. He'll remind you the blood of Jesus cleanses all sin (Ephesians 1:7), God's Word is eternal (Isaiah 40:8; Mark 13:31), and Jesus promised to be with you always (Matthew 28:20b). At the sound of God's Word, Satan will flee. He can never stay in the presence of the truth of God. Above all, cling to the promises of God. Remember, the power is in the Word!

APPLY Is there a promise in Scripture that's particularly precious to you?

_____

_____

_____

_____

God's Word brings stability and power into our lives, no matter the circumstances.

God's Work in Your Life

The second pillar is His work in your daily life. Do you remember the story of David and Goliath (1 Samuel 17)? If you're not familiar with it, it's a remarkable story. A young Israelite boy named David carried only a sling (similar to a slingshot) and five stones when he went into one-on-one combat against a monster of a man named Goliath, a champion soldier. As this young man prepared to go before Goliath, he said, *"The LORD who delivered me from the paw of the lion and the paw of the bear will deliver me from the hand of this Philistine"* (1 Samuel 17:37). David didn't claim victory based on his own merit. He looked back through his life and remembered times the Lord had delivered him. He used those memories to build his faith and to instill confidence in the frightened Israelite army around him.

Describe a time when the Lord delivered you.

_____

_____

_____

Sadly, we don't study this story enough as adults. We face "Goliaths" every day and we could learn much from David. We can have the same confidence as we meet our Goliaths, but first we must recognize God's hand in our lives.

As you look back through your life you might see Him in major events but it's harder to see Him in everyday life: the song played on the radio at just the right moment, the car you miraculously did NOT hit on the drive to work this morning, keeping your cool in that discussion with you-know-who . . . Each evening, think back through the noise of the day and try to pick out His still, small voice, caring for you. Praise Him for the large and the small works . . . and remember them. When Goliath strides onto the scene, begin to recount them and watch your confidence rise (and his tumble)!

APPLY If an unbelieving friend or family member asks you to prove Jesus is alive, what evidence can you describe to them of His work in your life (Philippians 1:6)?

_____

_____

_____

_____

_____

Some unbelievers say, "I'll believe in Jesus when I see Him!" They scoff at the Bible because they don't believe that this book is God's Word. One thing they can't argue with is God's work in your life. They can't argue with God's love revealed through your life. Your faith, lived out before them every day, is the evidence!

Faith: An unshakable foundation built by Jesus as we walk with Him, and supported by the indestructible truth of God's Word and His promises, as well as the undeniable evidence of His work in our lives. (Isaiah 28:16, Mark 13:3, Matthew 5:16)

This is the definition of faith we'll carry forward into this study on weathering the storms in our lives, as we take shelter beneath God's love and care.

FAITH-BUILDING

So often, our faith is battered and bruised by our circumstances. Perhaps it's shaken when we learn a loved one is battling a serious illness or as we watch dear young people make choices that could destroy their lives. Possibly it's rocked as we deal with the loss of a job or with a seemingly hopeless financial situation. Maybe you have one of those days when you feel as if someone stamped "Hit me, please!" on your forehead.

Have you walked through a crisis or had "just one of those days" that caused your faith to stumble? Will you give a brief description of the situation?

_____

_____

_____

_____

Why do we allow our faith to be rocked by our circumstances? For just a moment, step back to the day you met Jesus. It began with an amazing realization: God loves you so much He willingly sacrificed His only Son to wash away your sins and adopt you as His beloved daughter (Colossians 2:13–15; 1 John 3:1). Your confidence in His love led you to surrender your life to Him. Instantly, Jesus' blood cleansed you of a lifetime of sin and the Holy Spirit entered your heart. Second Corinthians 5:17 says you have become a new creation. Your first step of faith was based on God's love and, as the weeks, months, or years have passed, your faith has grown. What's been the cause of that growth? Has it been your intellect? Your church? Does your faith stand or fall depending on your circumstances?

Have you ever asked, "Why's my faith so weak?" Have you criticized yourself, "If only I'd had more faith I could've handled this better!"? I know I sure have! Sounds as if we're taking all the responsibility on ourselves, doesn't it? Hebrews 12:2 has good news for you!

> *"Let us fix our eyes on Jesus, the author and perfecter of our faith."*
> (Hebrews 12:2a)

 Why is it so important to fix our eyes on Jesus as we go through our daily lives?

_____

_____

_____

The first few words of Hebrews 12:2 tell us to keep our eyes fixed on Jesus. When we focus on our circumstances rather than on Jesus and His truth, we often feel overwhelmed and defeated. Do you try to deal with the situation yourself, rather than seek Jesus' guidance? When you focus on Jesus,

"Therefore, if anyone is in Christ, he is a new creation; the old has gone, the new has come!"
2 Corinthians 5:17

Do we really believe Hebrews 12:2, declaring Jesus to be the Creator of our faith?

you'll find He gives you the assurance that comes with knowing He's in control. He'll give you the strength to trust Him. When you seek His guidance, you'll find you're not running ahead of God and making the situation even worse. I can't even count how many times I've yelled for God's help because I'd first tried to deal with something myself and ended up in a much bigger mess!

During times of suffering, when my faith took a beating, I often attacked myself for being so weak. Why are we so hard on ourselves? I think it comes down to this fundamental question: Do we really believe Hebrews 12:2a, declaring Jesus to be the Creator of our faith? If so, when we attack ourselves for having a weak faith, we're really saying one of two things: Either we're accusing Jesus of doing a poor job of building and sustaining our faith, or we're saying we're doing a poor job of yielding ourselves to Him. There are no other options. Can Jesus do a poor job of anything? No! Do we ever yield to Him enough? No, we can always do better—but we can also acknowledge our desire to yield to Him and stop beating on ourselves.

Jesus knew what pitiful people He got when He died for us. Yet He did it willingly, *"for the joy set before Him"* (Hebrews 12:2b). Don't take responsibility for the strength of your faith. Leave it in Jesus' hands. Make it your goal to be His friend—to get to know Him as thoroughly as you can. Share every life experience, large and small, with Him. Love Him, laugh with Him, cry with Him. As you do, you'll hear the sound of faith-building in the background.

APPLY What does it mean to you to realize that Jesus, through the Holy Spirit within you, creates, increases, perfects, and sustains your faith?

_____

_____

_____

This doesn't mean you have absolutely nothing to do with the faith-building process. You do have a part; you can't just sit there while Jesus does all the work! In the Scriptures below, identify the things you can do to allow Jesus to build your faith.

"In everything, by prayer and petition, with thanksgiving, present your requests to God." (Philippians 4:6)

_____

_____

_____

"All Scripture is God-breathed and is useful for teaching, rebuking, correcting and training in righteousness." (2 Timothy 3:16)

_____

_____

_____

"I have hidden your word in my heart that I mightnot sin against you." (Psalm 119:11)

_____

_____

"Carry each other's burdens . . . encourage one another and build each other up . . . pray for each other." (Galatians 6:2; 1 Thessalonians 5:11; James 5:16)

_____

_____

You may look at these and think they sound deceptively simple. "Oh, I see! If I just pray, read the Bible, memorize a few verses, and fellowship with other believers . . . everything will be great!" Wait a minute—if you're doing all these and this Christian-walk thing is still awfully hard—join the club! Maintaining an intimate prayer life is hard, and have you really tried to understand Ezekiel lately? Answers to today's problems might seem unlikely in a book written more than 2,000 years ago.

Don't lose heart, dear one. Remember Jesus is working in you to accomplish these things (Philippians 1:6). He's center stage—you only have a small part. Let me give you an example from my life struggle. Because of my seizure disorder, I have a terrible memory; I've never been able to memorize Scripture. I remember some verses, snatches of others. I generally know if it's Old Testament or New, and I usually know if Jesus said it or not. That's about it. I never know what book it comes from, let alone chapter and verse. This always bothered me and I felt God was displeased with me because of it.

When I worked as a contractor at Johnson Space Center in Houston, a co-worker who sat next to me was of a different faith. Although he read the Bible, it wasn't the sacred text of his faith and he didn't believe Jesus was the only way for men to be saved. Occasionally, I'd be working away and he'd suddenly whirl around in his chair and say something like, "In Daniel XY:Z it says so and so. Here's what I think it means . . . What do you think?" I'd recognize the verse he quoted but wasn't quite sure I agreed with his interpretation. Bits of Scripture entered my mind, but I couldn't remember where to find them. I was afraid I'd sound stupid, so I'd say, "Let me check that out and get back to you."

I continually griped at God about these encounters, "God, how can you do this to me? You know I can't quote Scripture back to him. All I do is look stupid. Why can't You choose someone who's better at this?" One morning, during a complaint session, God decided enough was enough. He reminded me HE knew Scripture just fine because He'd written it. He took me to Matthew 4, Jesus' temptation in the desert by Satan. To answer Satan, Jesus quoted Old Testament Scripture—and you know what?! Jesus only quoted part of the verse and He didn't quote it perfectly. He didn't even give the reference! Not once did He say, "In Deuteronomy 8:3 it says . . ."

A simple truth was revealed to me as I read that passage: The power of God's Word is in the *words*! Of course the reference is important, but if I don't remember chapter and verse it should never prevent me from speaking His Word. If Jesus defeated Satan with words alone, then I could certainly carry on a discussion with my co-worker. More importantly, I could carry on a discussion with myself. When I face a difficult decision or when trials come, I can respond to the doubt and fear Satan brings into my mind with the power of God's Word. The phrases and words of Scripture I remember will bring me strength and peace. Jesus will keep His promise to you and to me. He'll use the Counselor (Holy Spirit), who lives within each of us, to remind us of His words (John 14:26), and then He'll use His words to build our faith.

"Being confident of this, that he who began a good work in you will carry it on to completion until the day of Christ Jesus."

Philippians 1:6

The power of God's Word is in the words!

FRUITS OF FAITH

One of my neighbors has an orange tree covered with fruit each fall. Because he waters and fertilizes the tree, the oranges are plump and sweet. It's a treat for us to pull them off the branches and enjoy their delicious flavor. God longs for us to share the sweetness of Jesus with those we know. That seems easy at first, doesn't it? We're so excited about our new life that we talk to everyone about it. But, to bear fruit throughout our lives, God knows our faith needs to mature through the work of the Holy Spirit. Let's examine our definition of faith to discover how God fortifies our faith and equips us to bear fruit in our lives.

Faith: An unshakable foundation built by Jesus as we walk with Him, and supported by the indestructible truth of God's Word and His promises, as well as the undeniable evidence of His work in our lives. (Isaiah 28:16, Mark 13:3, Matthew 5:16)

Security

I've lived in many areas of America: areas where tornadoes are common, areas where hurricanes batter the towns and cities, even areas where drought often causes destructive fires. But there's one place I don't ever want to live: an area prone to earthquakes. The ground's supposed to stay still! When I'm panicked by high winds and driving rain, I count on the solid, motionless ground beneath my feet. If the ground starts shaking and rolling my sense of stability disappears.

Nothing erases our joy as believers faster than the fear we're not secure in God's love. Those doubts cripple our lives and choke off our fruitfulness. We must stand on the unshakable foundation of God's Word, which confirms the security of our salvation. The Holy Spirit within us is the seal (proof) that our eternal lives begin at the moment we accept Jesus as our Savior (2 Corinthians 1:22). Jesus states this truth in a way we women can understand:

> *"I tell you the truth, no one can see the kingdom of God unless he is born again."* (John 3:3)

When we put our faith in Jesus, we're born into God's family; we become His daughters. I believe Jesus used the term born again on purpose. Once you're born, you can't be "un-born"! A baby can't crawl back into the womb. Any woman who's gone through the joy of labor and delivery will proclaim, "That ain't happenin'!" That baby is born—forever! When we accept Jesus, we're born to a new life (2 Corinthians 5:17). We can't be un-born.

Satan would love for us to doubt God's promise of a sure salvation, because it stifles our work for God. Once we accept Jesus, God will never reject us. Our salvation is everlasting—an unshakable foundation (Isaiah 45:17).

APPLY If you've doubted the security of salvation, how did God replace doubt with assurance?

_____

_____

_____

> **"[God] set his seal of ownership on us, and put his Spirit in our hearts as a deposit, guaranteeing what is to come."**
>
> **2 Corinthians 1:22**

Journey with Jesus

What a precious blessing! Jesus walks with us continually. God doesn't wind us up like robots and come back later to check the fruitfulness of our lives. Jesus walked where we walk and He walks with us now (Hebrews 4:14–16). He knows how hard it is for us to live out our Christian lives and to bear fruit in the world around us. It's especially hard when storms swirl around us. Even then, our response reveals the sweetness of Jesus to those around us. When they see the strength and peace in our lives, they'll wonder how we do it. What a great time to tell them of Jesus' peace!

> *"Peace I leave with you; my peace I give you. I do not give to you as the world gives. Do not let your hearts be troubled and do not be afraid."* (John 14:27)

This peace upheld Jesus as He faced the unbelief of His people. It strengthened Him as He faced the cross. His peace will carry us through each day, no matter what that day brings.

How has Jesus' presence given you peace as you face difficult days?

_____

_____

_____

_____

How could we survive without God's Word? It's a treasure chest, full of priceless gems that minister uniquely to each of us. The Holy Spirit brings it alive; it's like a chameleon, revealing new meanings as the circumstances in our lives change. The truth of His Word is consistent; it doesn't sway with the world's changing philosophies. We can stand on it when nothing else seems stable. It's never-changing.

> *"The grass withers and the flowers fall, but the word of our God stands forever."* (Isaiah 40:8)

God's Word reveals Jesus to us, shows us our sin, and proves God's love for us. As we study it, we learn more of Jesus' life. We discover the thoughts and behaviors that are pleasing to God. In those pages, we find the wisdom to make decisions that cause others to recognize God's guidance in our lives.

God's Word overflows with promises that assure us of His faithfulness. They give us the confidence we need to navigate the hard days. They provide the courage to resist the temptations that call to us from our old life. They assure us of God's presence and strength to enable us to make the right decisions when it would be easier to go with our instincts. Obeying God is not easy but His Word makes it possible.

Through every day, God's Word proves to be a teacher, a guide, and a yardstick by which to measure our actions. We can trust it to lead us in the right direction when we're not sure what to do.

> *"All Scripture is God-breathed and is useful for teaching, rebuking, correcting and training in righteousness."* (2 Timothy 3:16)

God's Word is consistent; it doesn't sway with the world's changing philosophies.

God's Word overflows with promises that assure us of His faithfulness.

How have the assurance of God's presence and the wisdom of His Word been your unshakable foundation?

_____

_____

_____

_____

Fruit to Share

When we choose to have confidence in God's love, to be assured of His presence, and to access His wisdom through the words of Scripture, we give the Holy Spirit the opportunity to transform us (Romans 12:2). He changes our thoughts and attitudes so they're more like those of Jesus. The Holy Spirit works from the inside out. A change in our hearts is reflected in a change in our behavior.

The changes that occur within us spill into our relationships and the way we respond to the situations we face. Galatians 5:22, 23 describes the fruit of the Spirit as *"love, joy, peace, patience, kindness, goodness, faithfulness, gentleness and self-control."* When these reside within us, it's impossible to carry on in our old ways.

Can we be filled with love and still feel a hatred that refuses to offer forgiveness? Sometimes we hang on to past anger, even though God wants us to forgive and to rebuild relationships. Love will create a desire to reach out, in spite of the risks. Can we value love and continue to show disrespect for those who don't fit in our circle? God asks us to be holy—set apart—from those around us in the way we treat others. We should always see the value in older people and respect their wisdom. We should never consider others unworthy because of their race or social status. In God's eyes all people have value, and He sacrificed His Son to confirm their worth.

Can we be at peace and yet attack with anger when we're hurt? Getting even is often more fun than letting the offense go. How often do we argue, just because it pampers our pride? Saying "I'm sorry" or "I was wrong" just doesn't work when we can't bear losing a battle. In each of these situations, God's call to peace demands we act differently than the world around us. As much as possible, we should encourage an environment of peace.

 How has the fruit of love and peace changed your thoughts and actions as you've become closer to God?

_____

_____

_____

Patience—oh, my, how I need patience! Only God can remove my tendency to criticize others when they don't live up to my expectations. The co-worker who needs the same explanation over and over—it's natural to lose patience and tell her to figure it out herself this time. Why not tell off a friend who forgot—again—about what you asked her to do? A little patience is hard to display when you think you have every right to react harshly. Remember: Where would you be if God lost His patience with you?

Where would you be if God lost His patience with you?

How will our words and actions change if our hearts overflow with kindness and goodness? Will we be eager to help someone when a little kindness will set their world back on its feet? Perhaps we'll hesitate to say a harsh word or repeat an unkind story when we focus on doing good. We can't measure the impact of praising people's strengths rather than pointing out their faults. No matter what we say or do, we should always be motivated by kindness and goodness (Ephesians 4:32).

Is there an occasion in your life when you didn't react with patience and kindness? How would you react to that same situation now?

_____

_____

_____

_____

Perhaps the hardest quality to express is faithfulness. So often a promise springs out of my mouth when I know I won't keep it. Perhaps I really meant to pray for that person but their name never crossed my mind again. Maybe my intentions were good but my record on following through is shameful. Words come easily, but actions take a commitment to stand by our promises. Even more important is the consistency between our words and our lives. Are we faithful to walk the path our own words define? Nothing is more harmful than a mouth that spouts virtuous living when we're unwilling to display it ourselves.

Integrity is defined as "doing the right thing, even if nobody is watching," (author unknown)." How has the Holy Spirit transformed you into a person of integrity?

When this fruit fills our hearts, it fills our lives. The changes in us shout "Jesus" to the world around us. The Holy Spirit's work causes us to respond in ways very different from the teachings of the world. He enables us to love those our world says are unworthy, as Jesus loved the outcasts of His day. He enables us to pray for and to forgive our enemies—even when they continue to attack us—as Jesus forgave those who crucified Him (Luke 23:3). He enables us to be obedient, even when every stubborn desire tempts us to disobey. He enables us to have thoughts and attitudes pleasing to Him. None of these is possible without the power of the Holy Spirit living within us.

> *"I [Jesus] am the vine; you are the branches. If a man remains in me and I in him, he will bear much fruit; apart from me you can do nothing."* (John 15:5)

> ### *Living like Jesus is impossible without the power of the Holy Spirit living within us.*

FAITH IN ACTION

Focus on Faith

DAY FOUR

Faith-talk is easy. Promises to God are easy to make. But when the storm clouds gather in our lives, talk is drowned out by the beating of our hearts and the confusion in our minds. We're no different from God's people in the past. Israelites in the Old Testament struggled with their faith when God seemed to abandon them. The faith of Christ's disciples collapsed around them when their expectations of Jesus didn't

> *Difficult times give God an opportunity to reveal to us the true strength of our faith.*

> *God doesn't expect us to obey Him when we're ready. He expects us to obey Him when He speaks.*

come true. Difficult times give God an opportunity to reveal to us the true strength of our faith.

Many times my faith has faltered, even when the circumstances were a result of my disobedience to God. I worked at Johnson Space Center for almost ten years. The last three years, I was assigned a very important project with many problems. To ensure it would meet its deadlines, I worked very long hours. I abandoned my prayer time in the mornings for a few extra minutes of sleep. I pulled out of most of the work I did at church. I neglected my husband and my extended family. I neglected my health in favor of my obsession with my project. Although all of us occasionally find ourselves under great stress at work, my situation persisted for three years with no relief in sight.

During my last year at work, God began to penetrate my thoughts with the conviction that I needed to quit my job. I was astonished and promptly told Him that was absurd and impossible. Everyone knew this project couldn't survive without me! The convicting thoughts continued for several months and I continued to stubbornly ignore them. One evening in late October, as I sat exhausted, His voice became so insistent I could no longer ignore it. Although I knew I should quit, I tried to bargain. My project was scheduled to ship to Kennedy Space Center in six months; I promised Him I'd quit after that. Ladies, bargaining with God never works. Two weeks after that evening, I was laid off.

I can't even begin to describe my shock and anger. My faith took a tumble, like water cascading off a cliff. We'd lose half our income—how could my husband and I pay the bills? My work was my life and my identity—who was I without my job? I didn't trust God with my finances, much less my life. My identity was not defined by Jesus, it was defined by my job. When God made no sense, my faith evaporated.

It wasn't until I'd been laid off for a few weeks that I realized how mentally, emotionally, and physically exhausted I was. I'm not sure how I survived the stress as long as I did. As I look back on those three years, several things stand out to me. God protected me from physical and mental collapse. He protected my marriage; my husband endured more than I ever realized. God gave me great grace by waiting for my stubborn heart to melt and come to agreement with Him on the "what," even though I refused to obey the "when." God doesn't expect us to obey Him when we're ready. He expects us to obey Him when He speaks.

There are many circumstances that cause our faith to tumble. In Scripture we find several instances when the faith of His people was tested. Those men and women responded to their situation—some with a weak faith, while others remained strong. I'm sure we'll see ourselves in the people we encounter in God's Word.

Victorious Faith
Often the most difficult time to remain strong is when God is silent. When we must wait for God's answer to our prayers or for His promises to be fulfilled, it's very hard to trust Him as the days, or even years, pass by. We must trust God's purpose and believe that His timing is perfect. The account of David's life (1 Samuel 16 – 1 Kings 2) describes David's response as he waited for God's promise to be fulfilled.

When David was in his teens, the prophet Samuel anointed him king of Israel (1 Samuel 16:13). He had every reason to expect he'd take the throne immediately, but that was not God's plan. David was forced to wait years for God's promise to be fulfilled, yet his faith remained strong.

Soon after his anointing, David was commissioned into the service of the reigning king, Saul. How frustrating it must have been to serve when he knew the office of king was promised to him. Yet he served Saul faithfully and humbly and never asserted his right to the throne. He was willing to wait for God.

As time passed, David was brave in battle and became a commander in the king's army. The Israelite people celebrated David's victories and gave him great admiration (1 Samuel 18: 6, 7). Saul's heart raged with jealousy; he believed the people honored David more than him. From that point on, Saul was David's enemy (1 Samuel 18:28, 29). He pursued David relentlessly and vowed to kill him.

David fled from Saul for years. I'm sure he cried out to God, afraid that God had forgotten him. I'm sure he longed to strike out to avenge the injustice done to him. But he recognized those years as part of God's plan. On more than one occasion, he had the opportunity to kill Saul but he refused to do so. He recognized God's sovereignty in the reign of Saul. To overthrow Saul would have been a denial of God's lordship. So David waited and trusted God to bring him to the throne when the time was right. Through those difficult years, God drew near to David and protected him.

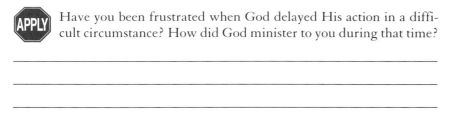 Have you been frustrated when God delayed His action in a difficult circumstance? How did God minister to you during that time?

_____

_____

_____

_____

In our world of instant gratification, none of us expects to wait. We have instant communication through cell phones and the Internet. Drive-thru service at banks, restaurants, and pharmacies has attempted to remove waiting from our experience. We're an impatient people. We need to recognize that God's perfect plan often requires us to wait. If we trust Him, He'll draw near to us and fill our waiting time with blessings. Often He uses that time to prepare us for days ahead.

When Saul died in a battle with the Philistines, David mourned his death rather than proclaim his right to the throne (2 Samuel 1). Even when Saul's son seized the throne, David didn't act. He was content to wait for God's timing and refused to challenge his rival. After many battles and many months, David was finally crowned the undisputed king of all Israel (2 Samuel 5:1–5).

David was almost forty years old when he was crowned king—more than twenty years after being anointed by Samuel. In all this time, through all the hardship, David never attempted to seize the throne. He chose to fully trust God and to wait for God's time.

God's perfect plan often requires us to wait.

How rich God's blessings will be if we accept His wisdom and His perfect timing.

What was God's purpose during those long years? David learned to serve humbly rather than to selfishly claim what should've been his. He became a great military leader by depending totally on God's protection, even when the odds seemed to be against him. He recognized that vengeance was the Lord's and refused to retaliate when treated unjustly. He faithfully followed God's guidance, even though it often seemed to bring even greater hardship.

All these lessons made David one of the greatest kings in Israel's history. His integrity and submission to God enabled him to unite divided Israel. His military leadership abilities enabled him to conquer Israel's enemies and to gain possession of all the land promised to Abraham centuries earlier. His acts of forgiveness and grace gained the undying admiration of all Israel. In the fullness of time, God blessed David and the nation of Israel with peace and prosperity.

APPLY How have the lessons God taught you in a season of waiting benefited you as you faced later challenges?

_____

_____

_____

_____

We can learn much from David. Even as his prayers were unanswered and God's promises remained unfulfilled, David chose to trust God's faithfulness. Unlike David, we often try to impose our timetable on God. Many times I have asked Him, "Do I need to send You a watch?" How rich God's blessings will be if we accept His wisdom and His perfect timing. We can trust His sovereignty in our situation and understand that the waiting is part of His perfect plan.

Defeated Faith
Many other circumstances cause us to lose faith. When we watch our situation worsen day by day, we may feel that God has withdrawn His hand of protection from our lives. Our faith's then overcome by fear and panic. This is just the situation faced by God's prophet Elijah (1 Kings 17ff).

Under King Ahab and his evil wife, Jezebel, Israel (the northern kingdom) had fallen into the worship of many false gods. They'd turned away from the one true God. Under God's direction, Elijah confronted the false prophets and challenged the power of the gods they served. In a great display of God's power, the false gods were destroyed and the false prophets were killed.

You can imagine the reaction of King Ahab to this defeat. His wife flew into a rage and ordered Elijah killed immediately. Although God had given him a great victory, Elijah panicked and fled in terror to hide in a cave on Mount Sinai. How could his faith be defeated by fear after seeing such a miraculous display of God's power?

How have you reacted when God gave you a victory in your storm but did not bring total deliverance?

_____

_____

As Elijah cowered in fear, God came to him and asked the question we often hear: *"What are you doing here, Elijah?"* (1 Kings 19:9). God wasn't referring to Elijah's physical location. He referred to Elijah's spiritual location. Elijah gave in to fear when he should've stood in his faith. He hid when he should've trusted God's power. He allowed his circumstances to defeat his faith.

God could've been disgusted with Elijah and left him in his fear. Instead, He came to Elijah and assured him of His presence. When Elijah felt all alone in his belief, God verified there were many other men who remained faithful to Him. God sought Elijah out and lifted him up. He strengthened Elijah and encouraged him to continue to serve God.

Have you ever taken a stand for God only to be overcome by despair and fear when He allowed things to fall apart? God will come to you, as He came to Elijah. He'll remind you of His promises. When we can't understand His actions, we can trust His character. When we're tempted to despair in the waiting, when we cower in fear, or when we are overcome by disappointment and frustration, we can trust His faithfulness. He is forever sovereign. We can trust His plans.

Was there a time when you feared that God had removed His protection? How did you respond? How did God minister to you during that time?

_____

_____

_____

_____

When we can't understand God's actions, we can trust His character.

TRUST GOD'S PLAN

Often, when we experience a crisis firsthand, our already weakened faith stumbles. We wonder, Has God's power been drained by the cries of the masses, leaving none for us in our time of need? All it takes is one of those days when everything goes wrong to make us feel as if God has abandoned us. It's so easy to lose sight of God's work in our lives and to lose hope in the victory Jesus gives us. First John 5:4 assures us we are overcomers when we trust God.

Faith is not an emotion. It doesn't rise and fall with the tides of life. It doesn't sway with the winds of circumstance. Our faith is built on the changeless character of God; it's the foundation of our lives. As we walk with Him, we learn more of Him and our faith becomes a substance that will stand the test of any circumstance.

The Lord God is sovereign in your life. His plan for your life is not only for today or this year. It's for the totality of your life and involves seasons of

Focus on Faith

DAY FIVE

"For everyone born of God overcomes the world. This is the victory that has overcome the world, even our faith."

1 John 5:4

blessing and seasons of suffering. The complete pattern—blessings and sufferings—is woven together to refine you and create the person He's designed you to be. As finite beings, we're unable to see the whole pattern; we're only able to see the threads running through our lives at the moment. We must trust that God sees the entire fabric and only allows into our lives what's needed to complete His perfect design.

APPLY As you look back on your life and the storms that have come and gone, how do you see the pattern God wove to create the person you are now and to bring you to the place where you are now?

_____

_____

_____

_____

Yet, when the storms come, doubts and questions flood our minds and our faith stumbles. "Do You know what's happening to me?" "Do You care?" "Where are You?" Do those questions sound familiar? They show we feel abandoned. We feel as if God's moved away from us and turned His eyes away from us.

Wait a minute! Where is God? Who looked away? We did! The questions we ask go much deeper than a matter of His presence. They express our doubts about His faithfulness. Is God still who we once trusted Him to be? God has not changed! As Hebrews 13:8 testifies, *"Jesus Christ is the same yesterday and today and forever."* He'll be the same a million tomorrows from now. God's love for you as His daughter has not changed, and will not change (1 Chronicles 16:34). When we experience this love and know God as the perfect Father, can we ever truly doubt His watch-care over us? Fix your eyes on Jesus; He's the only constant in this constantly changing world. He wants to be your Solid Rock.

Is Jesus your Solid Rock—or do you believe your life's just fine as it is? Satan works overtime to convince you your life should be nothing but glitz and glamour and fun. He tells you the world's wisdom is all you need. At some point you'll recognize the emptiness that alcohol, hours of work or partying, or self-actualization cannot satisfy. Do you struggle, trying to find guidance in worldly standards that change like shifting sand? Jesus is all-sufficient and unchanging. Only Jesus can provide what you need. Only Jesus can create and sustain your faith.

Faith—does this whole concept seem like a dream to you? Like a joke? Does God really love you as you are? I can hear your thoughts because I've thought them: "Forgiveness of all my sin? Yeah, right! You have no clue what I've done!" "God doesn't love me; I don't even love myself!"

Precious lady, I've said all those things—and more. I didn't believe God loved me or wanted to forgive me. One evening, God proved His love for me as I sat in my living room and listened to Billy Graham. I knew I was a sinner—I knew I'd been disobedient to God's standards. I believed I was too worthless for God to ever love me. But I didn't understand the depths of God's love.

Fix your eyes on Jesus; He's the only constant in this constantly changing world.

God's love is so strong He willingly sent His Son, Jesus, to live a perfect life on earth and then to die on the cross. The penalty for disobedience to God is death—not just physical death but eternal spiritual death. Even though Jesus was sinless, He willingly died on the cross to pay the death penalty we deserve for our sins. He didn't die for a select group. He didn't die for certain sins, having decided others were too terrible to forgive. Jesus died for all people and to offer forgiveness for all sin.

Even more wonderful, Jesus' life didn't end on the cross. After three days in the grave, God's power resurrected Him—raised Him to eternal life. Jesus' eternal life is the promise of our eternal life—life with God forever.

Have you accepted God's gift of forgiveness and eternal life? If so, how have these gifts grown even more precious to you as time has passed?

_____

_____

_____

_____

> ## *"For God so loved the world that he gave his only Son, so that everyone who believes in him will not perish but have eternal life."*
>
> ## *John 3:16*

But forgiveness and eternal life aren't automatic. Each of us must believe who Jesus is and ask for God's forgiveness. Each of us must believe in Jesus' resurrection and the promise of eternal life.

Dear one, Jesus died for you. His death provides forgiveness for all your sin and His resurrection is the promise of your eternal life (1 John 2:25). Even now, if you pray and ask for God's forgiveness, He will wash away every sin. He'll send the Holy Spirit to live within you, and will give you eternal life (Galatians 4:6, John 3:16).

If you've never done so, the prayer below will help you ask Jesus into your life:

Lord God, I know I'm a sinner. I believe Your Son, Jesus, died on the cross for the forgiveness of my sins, and then was resurrected to give me eternal life. I ask Jesus to come into my heart as my Savior. Thank You, Lord, for loving me. Amen.

If you said this prayer, giving your life to Jesus, let someone know. Are there dear friends who encouraged you to participate in this study? Let them know of your decision to believe in Jesus. I encourage you to begin attending a church near your home, perhaps with other ladies in this study or with family members. As soon as possible, talk to a pastor and tell him of your decision. Allow him to guide you in the next steps of faith. God bless you and keep you.

Notes

2

Jesus Is Trustworthy

How wonderful is our Lord! Listen to the words of Exodus 34:6:

The LORD, the LORD, the compassionate and gracious God, slow to anger, abounding in love and faithfulness.

Compassionate . . . What a beautiful word! Jesus revealed God's compassion as He stood on the hill overlooking Jerusalem, and desired to gather her people into His arms (Matthew 23:37). Throughout the ages, God has shared the pain and sorrow of His people. Praise God for His loving compassion!

Gracious: "full of grace." As believers, the grace of God overflows our hearts and lives every day. The grace of God is defined as "undeserved favor." Because of God's grace, we are offered the gifts of salvation and eternal life—gifts we certainly do not deserve and can never repay.

Slow to anger . . . Aren't you happy about that one?! I know He would've struck me with lightning several times if He were not slow to anger. How many times have you known you should've received His discipline, but He responded with patience instead?

Abounding in love . . . Can you imagine the infinite love that took Christ to the cross to die for sinful men and women? This kind of love is beyond our understanding, yet without it we would be lost.

Abounding in faithfulness . . . What God says, He will do! His promises are true—we can depend on that. How many times do we make promises and then forget all about them? God *never* forgets. He's faithful to keep every promise in His Word.

As you go through the lessons this week, God's desire is for you to recognize He's the only One worthy of your trust.

Jesus is Trustworthy

DAY ONE

The world offers easy solutions; God often requires us to do the hard thing.

A QUESTION OF CONFIDENCE

Shouldn't it be easy to trust a caring, loving God who responds to us with compassion, patience, grace, and faithfulness? When we seek strength and guidance to navigate through the storms of life that assault us, whose words command our confidence—those of the world or those we read in God's Word? The world offers easy solutions; God often requires us to do the hard thing. It's easier to listen to earthly guidance than to trust God. Often society's wisdom carries more authority in this world than does God's Word.

When have you sought the advice of friends to guide you instead of going to God's Word? What was the result?

_____

_____

_____

_____

Listen to the writer of Hebrews proclaim Jesus' supreme authority in guiding us through life's difficult situations: He is our *great high priest*. No one's greater, no one's higher. No other's wisdom or teaching commands our confidence or guides our responses to the circumstances we face.

> *"Therefore, since we have a great high priest who has gone through the heavens, Jesus the Son of God, let us hold firmly to the faith we profess. For we do not have a high priest who is unable to sympathize with our weaknesses, but we have one who has been tempted in every way, just as we are—yet was without sin. Let us then approach the throne of grace with confidence, so that we may receive mercy and find grace to help find grace to help us in our time of need."* (Hebrews 4:14–16)

Cherish the words of this passage. Jesus can *sympathize with our weaknesses*. He was *tempted in every way* we are—*yet was without sin*. Even now, He's seated by His Father showering us with *mercy and grace*. We'll look at the fullness of these blessings in the days to come, but first let's examine Jesus' role as our High Priest.

The idea of a high priest has little meaning to Christians today. Even though we recognize Jesus as our Savior, we usually don't call on Him as our Priest.

To understand why Jesus' authority to direct our lives rests in this position, let's examine the role of the priests, especially the high priest, at the time this passage was written.

An Earthly Priesthood
The priesthood was critical to the Jewish people because their access to God and to His forgiveness was mediated by the priests. The people depended upon the priests to teach God's Word, to lead them in worship, and most importantly, to offer the sacrifices that cleansed them from sin.[3] The high priest was God's representative; he communicated God's will to the people. He was also the advocate for the people before God; He offered the sacrifices of atonement.

The people in Jesus' time didn't have a scroll of God's Word they carried home from the synagogue after worship. They depended on the priests to teach them God's laws and to be an example of righteous living (Leviticus 10:10, 11). Unfortunately, the priests in Jesus' time were more interested in status and political gain than in being God's messengers.

What a privilege it is to hold God's Word in our hands, to open it and receive wisdom and guidance! But with that privilege comes responsibility. How often do we depend on our preachers and teachers to explain God's Word without searching out its truths for ourselves? How many of us are oppressed by man's legalism and the "I'm right, you're wrong" philosophy? God's Word brings us into the fullness of a relationship with Him. It frees us from legalism and to the joy of service. Immerse yourself in His Word and allow it to bless and enrich you!

How has God's Word blessed you with wisdom and guidance?

_____

_____

_____

_____

For the Jewish people, God's forgiveness wasn't "just a prayer away." They viewed God as an angry God who demanded the spilling of blood to protect them from His wrath. They confessed their sins and received His forgiveness through an elaborate system of sacrifices. The priests stood every day to offer sacrifices for sins committed by individuals.

The most important sacrifice of the year occurred on the Day of Atonement. Only on this day was the high priest allowed to enter the Most Holy Place to confess the sins of the entire nation in God's presence (Leviticus 16:32–34; Hebrews 9:7). Within the holy sanctuary of the temple, the high priest offered sacrifices to receive God's forgiveness for the sins of the people. This solemn ceremony was repeated each year to seek God's forgiveness for the sins of the past year.[4]

Because of Jesus' perfect sacrifice—for all sin, for all time—we no longer need approach God through ritual sacrifices. Jesus tore away the barrier between man and God and we are able to approach God with confidence and be assured of His forgiveness (Matthew 27:51; Hebrews 10:19, 20).

Jesus's perfect sacrifice is for all sin, for all time.

APPLY What joy and confidence do you gain from knowing you can come to God at any time for forgiveness?

_____

_____

_____

_____

Through times of both rejoicing and despair, Jesus is the fullness of God and our perfect High Priest.

A Heavenly High Priest

In Jesus, we have *"a great high priest who has gone through the heavens."* In all ways He is the supreme High Priest. Earthly priests died, and a parade of men held the office of high priest; Jesus' priesthood is holy and eternal (Hebrews 9:25, 26). Earthly priests adapted God's truth to meet their needs; Jesus' teachings are true—He is the Truth (John 14:6)! His words were not man's words; they came from His Father (John 7:16). Countless times He said, *"I tell you the truth . . ."* We can trust His words to guide our lives.

Earthly priests compromised to accomplish their goals; Jesus' life is the perfect model of righteousness. We only have to look to Jesus to see Him as the perfect expression of God and His truth. He's the perfect expression of God's wisdom—His sinless life teaches us how to walk in righteousness. He's the perfect expression of God's compassion—He reached out with healing and kindness to those around Him. He's the perfect expression of God's mercy—His death on the cross delivers us from the punishment we deserve. He's the perfect expression of God's grace—He freely offers us rich blessings and the gift of eternal life. Through times of both rejoicing and despair, Jesus is the fullness of God and our perfect High Priest.

The sacrifices offered by the priests had to be repeated time and time again to secure God's mercy. Imperfect men performing an imperfect sacrifice, over and over again. Jesus appears before God as the eternal High Priest who voluntarily offers His body and blood as the perfect, once-for-all sacrifice. Through His shed blood, each of us receives forgiveness of all our sins and complete access to God as our Father. Jesus is the complete and final Sacrifice.

"All authorities and powers are submitted to Him" . . . Isn't that exciting? Jesus is the perfect image of God and His priesthood is eternal. Now that He's risen and is seated at the right hand of the Father, He's crowned in glory and honor (Hebrews 2:9). The authority of an earthly high priest pales in comparison!

No matter what we face, Jesus reigns in authority over it. He conquers Satan's grip of sin and our fear of death by defeating them on the cross and giving us eternal life. He reigns over our experiences—both blessings and difficulties. No situation is out of His control and no experience catches Him off guard. Jesus reigns supreme!

Overcoming Weaknesses

The older I get, the weaker I become! I wake up several times during the night; therefore, I'm tired all the time. My knees hurt when I go up and down stairs. Exercise? Forget it! The only bright spot is that my memory's failing, so I don't remember all these aches and pains from one time to the next.

Did Jesus face any of these problems? Sure, we know Jesus left His heavenly throne and crawled into human skin but none of us can grasp the contrast between Jesus' heavenly home and His earthly existence. He stepped down from a throne to a seat on the hard ground. He gave up glory for ridicule. He left awesome power to feel all the aches and pains of man's frailness.

Disappointment, discouragement, exhaustion, aches and pains—many of us struggle just to get to the end of the day, and with our sanity intact. The stress of our day-to-day lives wears us down. How can Jesus relate to the pressures we face? After all, life was much simpler 2,000 years ago, wasn't it? How can Jesus understand the struggles of our "modern" lives? Read again the beautiful words of Hebrews 4:15:*"For we do not have a high priest who is unable to sympathize with our weaknesses."*

Jesus tasted all of life. He experienced the total vulnerability of infancy, dependent on others to meet His basic needs. He viewed His Creation through the curious eyes of a two-year-old, tasting and questioning everything. As a four-year-old, did He beg His mother for a cookie right before dinner? As a young teen, His heart probably leaped when a cute girl walked by. We can imagine His hands had calluses. He probably even had the dreaded "bad hair days." Yes, Jesus was fully God, but He was also fully human (John 1:1, 2, 14).

"Sympathize with our weaknesses." Because He was human, Jesus faced the same stresses we face. Did He ever get up in the morning, so tired He wasn't sure He could make it through another day? Was He ever disappointed or frustrated with the people around Him? Physical and emotional exhaustion—He felt it all. He not only understands the weaknesses that plague us—He experienced them.

A Day-to-Day Struggle
How many of us can identify with Jesus as He dealt with the strains of each day? He was often exhausted, hungry, and stressed by His work to no end. Did His head ache after a day walking in the blinding sun? I'm sure His feet were sore from hours spent walking on dirt roads littered with stones. He had no home of His own, no place to find rest and shelter from the sun and the rain. Many mornings He must have been exhausted after spending the night on the ground with only His cloak for warmth and a stone for His pillow. Did He ever wonder about His next meal?

Jesus chose to share the frailty of human life with us. Are we exhausted by a night of tossing and turning? Jesus surely was uncomfortable on the hard ground. Many of us deal with physical pain every day. We can only guess how His body ached from traveling down the dusty road day after day. A few of us may have huddled on a street corner to escape the cold and the

Jesus was fully God, but He was also fully human.

Jesus chose to share the frailty of human life with us.

rain, with no hope of a meal—today or tomorrow. Jesus understands! Each sunrise brought the uncertainty of where He might sleep and what He might eat.

What uncertainties fill your life? How has God been your security?

_____

_____

_____

_____

Rest—how He must have needed rest! Everywhere He went, crowds of people enveloped Him. How did He escape the cries of the needy that echoed around Him continually? Did He want to just shrug off His responsibilities and find some peace and quiet?

Even though Jesus was seldom physically alone, I'm sure He was often emotionally alone. Although people hounded Him, they only wanted what He could give them. Very few truly loved Him. He wasn't even accepted in His hometown (Luke 4:14–24). Did His heart ache for companionship?

Peace and quiet—doesn't that sound wonderful? We're all assaulted by demands—at work, at home—it never ends. As soon as we find a minute to ourselves, the phone rings! Voices come at us from everywhere, draining us of our energy. Yet many of us hunger for a true friend—someone we can confide in and who will love us, no matter what we say or do. We crave a girlfriend who understands the pressures of being a wife and mother or of being a single woman making her way alone.

Jesus understands! His life teaches us how to cope with the madness. Over and over again, Jesus retreated to the mountains to be with His Father. Alone with God, with the sounds of His Creation drowning out the uproar of daily life, His Father calmed Jesus' spirit and ministered to Him. Jesus could confide His deepest feelings and receive the strength and encouragement He needed.

Jesus is the Companion who never leaves us.

APPLY Rest, peace and quiet, companionship . . . Read Psalm 23 and describe how God meets your needs.

_____

_____

_____

Only Jesus can meet our deepest needs. Only Jesus truly understands our struggles. He is the Companion who never leaves us. He shares in our laughter, and views our tears with compassion. God waits for us to come to Him—to receive the peace that passes all understanding (Philippians 4:7). He longs to draw us away from the chaos and to lead us beside quiet waters. He longs to anoint us with the oil of His love. Climb into His lap and rest in His grace.

Defeating Discouragement
Often the time at which we are the weakest is when discouragement knocks at our heart's door. Not only does Jesus understand the day-to-day struggles

we face, He also understands our battle with hopelessness. We become discouraged for many reasons. Maybe we have "one of those days." Perhaps we watch our dreams fade in the harsh light of reality. When our prayers go unanswered, life seems too hard to bear. Discouragement is one of Satan's most powerful tools. If he can rob us of our hope, then we fall into his trap. Jesus experienced discouragement and overcame it.

When Jesus was twelve, his family traveled to Jerusalem to celebrate Passover. After the festival, Jesus remained in the temple talking to the teachers, who were amazed at His wisdom and knowledge (Luke 2:47). When Jesus' parents found Him there, His words signaled a shift in His focus: *"Didn't you know I had to be in my Father's house?"* (Luke 2:48, 49). His relationship and allegiance shifted from His earthly parents to His heavenly Father.

As Jesus lingered in the temple, did God reveal to Him the calling on His life? When He returned home, did He excitedly long to begin His ministry? We assume He did, but the reality of life interrupted Jesus' plans, as it often does ours.

Joseph, Jesus' human father, isn't mentioned in the Gospels after the trip to Jerusalem when Jesus was twelve years old. It's possible he died when Jesus was still a young man.[5] If so, as the eldest son, tradition dictated that Jesus become the head of the family and take over His father's business. Try to imagine how His life changed from days of anticipation of beginning His heavenly Father's work, to the years after Joseph's death, when He was "head of household."

Instead of leaving to begin His ministry as He might have dreamed, He found Himself responsible for supporting His family. Breadwinner, father figure, head of the house, spiritual leader . . . all the time dealing with His own grief, frustration, and disappointment. Did His father's customers readily accept Jesus, or did they take their carpentry work elsewhere? Was family life smooth? Were there many times when the phrase "You are not my father!" echoed off the walls as He disciplined His younger brothers and sisters? Did Jesus lose sight of His mission as these years of turmoil went by?

 As you think through these years of Jesus' life, what disappointments and crises might Jesus have faced similar to those you face today? How does this change your view of Him as *your* High Priest, One who is able to minister to you and intercede for you in all your specific storms of life?

_____

_____

_____

_____

Put yourself in Jesus' place for a moment. Discouragement and disappointment could have led to anger, bitterness, and rebellion. How could Jesus have possibly dealt with these years of storms and emotion and remained *sinless*? Yet He did just that!

Jesus dealt with years of storms and emotion and remained sinless.

My mind is filled with the lyrics of the precious hymn "The Solid Rock" (Lyrics [see Appendix A] by Edward Mote, *circa* 1834. Music by William B. Bradbury, 1863): "My hope is built on nothing less than Jesus' blood and righteousness." Our hope and confidence when we are facing life's storms are based only on the righteousness of Jesus. He walked where we walk. He searched for the sun but His trials oppressed Him as though they were dark, heavy clouds. He felt circumstances sting like bitter wind and rain on His face. Through it all, He remained sinless.

He understands every emotion that swirls through our minds and every fear that grips our hearts. He knows the path through every storm and can lead us safely through, because He has experienced what we experience. We must learn, as the hymn goes on to say: "On Christ the Solid Rock I stand, All other ground is sinking sand".

If we think about Jesus in this new way, as a man who lived through the struggles of a human life, it becomes easy to accept Him as our High Priest, the One who's able to identify with the storms we face. He is our perfect Advocate, seated at the right hand of the Father, interceding for us (Luke 22:69; Hebrews 7:25). Seated at the right hand of the Father—and yet here with us every moment. Here to comfort, to strengthen, and to guide. His presence warms us when we're cold with fear and softens our hearts when they're hardened with anger. His gentle voice whispers the truth of Scripture into our minds to break apart the doubt and chaos and to guide us when we've lost our way.

Jesus can sympathize with your weaknesses, even in His perfection. It was for this reason that He was born and lived on the earth as a human. He could have suddenly appeared in Jerusalem a few days before Passover, riled up the Sanhedrin, and been crucified for the sins of all mankind—short and to the point. But it was important to Him that He experience life as you live it, with all its vulnerabilities and tender spots, so He can serve you perfectly as your High Priest. Who can better enable you to conquer your weakness than the One who has walked the path before you?

CONQUERING SIN

The writer of Hebrews proclaims that Jesus was *"tempted in every way, just as we are—yet was without sin"* (4:15). That may be true for God's Son, but for us it should read "tempted in every way and sinning almost every time!" My Mom used to tell me I could trip on thin air. That's an exaggeration, but I certainly seem to trip over Satan's snares time and time again. How can I be sure Jesus identifies with my struggles? How can He guide me safely through Satan's minefield?

"Tempted in every way, just as we are" . . . Jesus overcame every temptation. He was rejected by His own people, yet didn't respond with anger. He lived in poverty yet never sought comforts and possessions. He was attacked by the religious leaders of His time but He never watered down the truth in an attempt to be more popular.

Jesus' presence warms us when we're cold with fear and softens our hearts when they're hardened with anger.

Jesus is Trustworthy

His holiness was repulsed by sin—we are often attracted to it. He remained sinless—we often stumble. Jesus was assaulted by Satan's power in a way we can never understand. Before Satan's temptations become too painful, we yield to his attack. Jesus never succumbed to his wiles, and Satan's attacks became more and more violent, beyond what we will ever experience. Through it all, Jesus emerged victorious. His victory over sin becomes ours when we surrender our lives to Him.

The Desert of Suffering
The desert: dry, desolate, full of agony. We often stagger through a desert of our own making. The consequences of our sin can parch our lives and leave us thirsty for relief. Let's follow Jesus into the desert and discover the path of God's deliverance.

When we read Matthew 3:13–17, the desert seems far away. As Jesus stepped into the waters of the River Jordan, the scene that unfolds before us is as thrilling as any moment in a movie. The crowds who gathered at the river that day were stunned to see God's light fall on Jesus. They must have gasped as they heard God's voice proclaim, "This is my Son!" Imagine the headlines in the next issue of the Galilee Gazette: Hundreds Hear God's Voice! Or maybe: God Proclaims Jesus His Son! Imagine the crowds gathering around Him after such a miraculous event! What a victorious start to Jesus' ministry!

But the next part of God's plan was very different. He led Jesus into the desert to be tempted by Satan. Even more miraculous, Jesus willingly followed! Why must Jesus' ministry begin in the barren desert? Did God need to test Jesus' obedience? Of course not—Jesus was Holy God wrapped in man's clothing. God's aim wasn't to test Jesus—it was to teach us. Through Jesus' temptation, we learn the weapons that will defeat Satan.

Satisfy Our Desires

> *Then Jesus was led by the Spirit into the desert to be tempted by the devil. After fasting forty days and forty nights, he was hungry. The tempter came to him and said, "If you are the Son of God, tell these stones to become bread." Jesus answered, "It is written: 'Man does not live on bread alone, but on every word that comes from the mouth of God'."* (Matthew 4:1–4)

Jesus was hungry. Satan seized on this time of hunger to challenge Jesus. The word "if" used here would be better translated "because".[6] Satan did not question Jesus' identity as God's Son. He tempted Jesus to rely on His own power to meet His needs. It's as though Satan said, "Because you are God's Son, there's no reason for you to be hungry. You have the power to change these rocks into bread."

Satan attacked Jesus at a time of great physical weakness, hoping Jesus would put His needs before God's will. Why would it have been wrong for Jesus to transform the stones into bread? He was a man; men need food. He was God; He could provide whatever He needed. Why not? The question was not *whether* Jesus would be fed, the question was *how* He would be fed. For Jesus to use His supernatural powers to meet His needs would violate God's plan: Jesus was to live as a man, trusting God to supply all He needed.

This temptation to satisfy our needs and desires is the basis for many sins that impact us and those around us. We crave the possessions and status of

Jesus' victory over sin becomes ours when we surrender our lives to Him.

In all circumstances, God's Word is our strength and our shield.

our neighbors. An alcoholic's body cries out for a drink. Sexual desire becomes overwhelming when tempted by an office romance. The thrill of gambling becomes addictive. Many people have lost jobs and families because they couldn't resist temptation. Satan attacks us at our point of weakness, hoping we will satisfy our hunger rather than be obedient to God.

When faced with these cravings, how do we resist them? When Satan dangles temptation in front of us, how do we keep our focus on God? Jesus gives us the answer: We live by the Word of God. God's powerful words will enable us to resist Satan's charms. The promises in His Word will give us the faith we need to trust Him to meet our needs, even when we're tempted to meet them in our own way and our own time. In all circumstances, God's Word is our strength and our shield.

 Is there a desire that threatens to control your life? If so, how is God's Word bringing you victory?

_____

_____

_____

Presume God's Protection

Then the devil took him to the holy city and had him stand on the highest point of the temple. "If you are the Son of God," he said, "throw yourself down. For it is written: 'He will command his angels concerning you, and they will lift you up in their hands, so that you will not strike your foot against a stone.'" Jesus answered him, "It is also written: 'Do not put the Lord your God to the test.'" (Matthew 4:5–7)

"For it is written" . . . Imagine the nerve, quoting Scripture to God Himself! Satan recited words from Psalm 91:11, 12. He was very careful to pull out only the words that suited his purpose. He neglected to say God's protection has a condition: *"If you make the Most High your dwelling"* (Psalm 91:9).

Satan's temptation was twofold. First, did Jesus believe God would fulfill His promises? Satan tempted Jesus to prove God's faithfulness through a deliberate action that would force God to keep His promise. Satan asked: "Can God pass the test?" If Jesus doubted God on this day, He would doubt God's promise of resurrection when He faced death on the cross. His doubt would have led to His disobedience—and the spotless sacrifice necessary to secure our redemption would have been tarnished.

How often do we doubt God's promises? How often do we refuse to obey Him because we do not believe His promise to enable us? I often rush out in my own strength and then claim His promises of presence and power. We cannot force God to prove Himself to us. He demands faith and obedience. His promises are valid only if we dwell in Him and walk in His will.

Second, Satan claimed that God must respond to Jesus' demands, no matter how foolhardy His actions were. Who was Lord and Master, Jesus or God? Must Jesus obey God or must God obey Jesus? Satan tempted Jesus to accomplish God's will through His own methods and demand that God respond as promised.

Satan's lies are alive and well today. Many believe God's promises are indeed commands God must follow, no matter the circumstance. We step out of His will and still expect His blessing and protection. Why are we shocked when sexual license leads to an unwanted pregnancy? Are we angry at God when our indulgences lead to illness? Are we perplexed when He doesn't bless our work if we serve Him in our own way rather than His? God's promises are not credit cards to be used as we please!

Jesus recognized Satan's lie and again defeated him with God's Word. By forcing God to act, Jesus would challenge God to prove Himself. By stepping out of God's will, Jesus would force God to meet His demands. Jesus declared that it's a sin to test God—to test His faithfulness or to test His sovereignty.

When have you doubted God's promises or demanded He obey your will?

_____

_____

_____

_____

How precious are God's promises to those of us who walk in His will! Over and over we find Him faithful. Hardship and suffering are not a sign of God's broken promises, although Satan tries to convince us of just that. God's Word is sure and true, even though His timing doesn't always match ours. God uses difficult times to teach us; in the desert place, we experience the richness of each promise and the security of His presence.

The Safety of Compromise

> *"Again, the devil took him to a very high mountain and showed him all the kingdoms of the world and their splendor. 'All this I will give you,' he said, 'if you will bow down and worship me.' Jesus said to him, 'Away from me, Satan! For it is written: Worship the Lord your God, and serve him only.'"* (Matthew 4:8–10)

This was perhaps the most challenging temptation of all. Surely Jesus knew the glory waiting for Him on the other side of the cross. Not only would He be Savior but He would be King! He knew He would reign over all peoples and nations; His enemies would become His footstool and His kingdom would be eternal. But . . . God's plan required that Jesus face extreme suffering and death on the cross before these truths would become reality.

Satan offered Jesus the promised throne of glory now. No suffering, no agony, no death. It all could be His—for a price: His allegiance. Would Jesus remain submitted to His Father's plan, a path of pain, or would He turn His allegiance to Satan and grasp glory now? Why must He travel through the agony when God's purposes could be accomplished painlessly? Surely this "small compromise" would be understandable.

Praise God—Jesus never wavered! He set His face toward Jerusalem, determined to be obedient to His Father, even to death. To avoid the cross would be to condemn all people to eternal damnation. Before Jesus could be King, He had to be Savior.

God's promises are not credit cards to be used as we please!

Before Jesus could be King, He had to be Savior.

The way of compromise is always much smoother than the way of obedience to God. Satan whispers to us, "Compromise your standards. When you blend in with the world, your opportunities to witness will be greater." He tempts pastors, "Soften the truth and more people will come to hear God's Word and to accept Jesus as Lord." To compromise God's standards is to shift our allegiance from God to the Enemy. God's purposes can only be accomplished by God's methods.

The lure of compromise is strong. The easy path is so seductive. We can't linger, thinking it over. We must respond immediately, as Jesus did, *"Away from me, Satan!"* Begin to worship God and Satan will flee. The power of God's Word will overcome Satan every time.

APPLY Have you experienced a situation in which the temptation to compromise was strong? How did you respond and what was the result?

_____

_____

_____

_____

_____

Because Jesus met Satan face-to-face and defeated him, He can defeat the grip of sin on our lives. We are no longer prisoners to sin, because He broke the chains. When we do fall, He lifts us up, dusts us off with His forgiveness, then teaches us through the consequences we experience. Because He used God's Word to resist Satan's temptations, He teaches us that God's Word is the shield protecting us from Satan. Cling to Him in faith and His victory becomes yours!

Jesus is Trustworthy

Jesus will never leave you to walk through the storm alone.

Our Good Shepherd

When the storms come, it's such a blessing to have a friend who knows what we are going through, someone who can walk by our side and encourage us. Dear one, Jesus is walking by your side! He has felt—and conquered—the fear and pain you feel. He desires to cry with you and to comfort you.

Who can strengthen and guide us better than the One who has walked the same path? He understands every weakness we have and every temptation we face. Even now Jesus stands before God and prays that God will deliver you through the hard days.

Yes, Jesus is on His throne but He is also in our hearts. He longs to travel with us, to take every step with us. He knows the way and He will strengthen us and guide us as we try to negotiate the wilderness. Never cease to be amazed at His presence with you, at His tenderness and love for you! You are a priceless gift, given to Him by His Father. He will never leave you to walk through the storm alone.

The Work of the Shepherd

In John 10, Jesus uses two parables to reveal the intimate relationship God desires to have with each of us:

> *"He calls his own sheep by name."* (John 10:3)
> *"I know my sheep and my sheep know me."* (John 10:14)

Because shepherds were very common in Jesus' day, many in His audience understood the picture painted by His words. Sheep are not the most intelligent animals; they are easily led into danger. It makes sense Jesus compares us to sheep, doesn't it?

Even in a large herd of sheep, the shepherd knew each one and often had a unique call for each sheep. If one of the sheep strayed from the herd, the voice of the shepherd would bring it back to safety. The sheep knew the call of their master and responded to him.[7]

Your Father knows your name. He knows you—your personality, your favorite color, your laugh, the taste of your tears, even the number of hairs on your head (Luke 12:7). (For some of us, He has to recount by the minute!) He loves each strength and each weakness; He fit them all together to make you the unique person you are. As your heavenly Father, He sees you as you are—and as you will be when He has completed the work He's begun in you (Philippians 1:6).

Genesis 1:31 says that God sees you, His creation, as *very good*. What goodness do you see in yourself?

_____

_____

_____

The desire of your Father's heart is for you to come to know Him more deeply as each day passes. He gives you His Word to allow you to learn of Him through His truth and through His Son's life. He gives you full access to Him through prayer, so you can share your life with Him. Every moment we spend with Him makes us more and more sensitive to His voice. When He calls out to us to bring us back to Him, we recognize His voice and respond to Him.

Do you recognize God's voice? When has He called out to you and how did you respond?

_____

_____

_____

_____

God jealously guards your life so the only experiences entering in are those that will bring you closer to His goal: transforming you into the image of His Son (Romans 8:29). Jesus described this watch-care beautifully in John 10:7 when He said, *"I tell you the truth, I am the gate for the sheep"* (John 10:7).

Every moment we spend with God makes us more and more sensitive to His voice.

Only if the storm accomplishes God's purposes, will He allow it to enter our lives.

The people who heard Him knew He was describing the willingness of the shepherd to guard his sheep with his very life. Each evening, the shepherd rounded up his flock and secured them for the night, usually into a cave. The cave didn't have a gate, so the shepherd would lie across the opening to sleep. In this way, the sheep were unable to stray without waking the shepherd. Wild animals were unable to enter the pen to attack the sheep.[8]

As our Shepherd, Jesus lies across the gate to our lives. We're unable to stray out of God's will into danger without His knowledge, and we're allowed to go only so far before He intervenes. In the same way, no storm enters our lives without first passing through Jesus. The impact of the storm is measured: Will it bring glory to God? Will it refine us, bringing us closer to the image of Christ? Will it deepen our relationship with God and teach us more of Him? Only if the storm accomplishes God's purposes, He will allow it to enter our lives.

Keep your eyes on the Shepherd as you walk through the storm. Have faith that its intensity is perfectly matched to His purpose. Be honest with Him about your thoughts and fears, but take time to ask Him what you can learn and how you can grow through the experience. The storm must be endured; do not waste it by missing the blessing contained within.

APPLY How are you encouraged, knowing Jesus only allows storms to enter your life if they will glorify God and mature your faith?

_____

_____

_____

_____

Going It Alone
I confess that too often my definition of trusting Jesus sounds like this: "Jesus, I've devised my own plan. I pray for You to give me success and I will glorify You." That's not trusting Jesus! That's trusting myself and asking Him to bless me! Throughout our own lives and throughout Scripture we see the results of going it alone, sheep without a shepherd. When dark days come, we try to find our way through with the feeble light of our own wisdom. We try to resist temptation in our own strength. Our plans always lead to disaster. Our strength will always fail us.

Doubt, compromise, impatience . . . we all stumble into these traps. But what snares us most often is our refusal to wait for our Shepherd's guidance and His perfect timing. We, as sheep, think we know more than the Shepherd. When God takes too long, we are masters at devising a plan of our own. Waiting on God goes against our nature.

Genesis 16 reveals the dangers of our own schemes. God promised Abram a son, but many years passed and nothing happened (Genesis 15:1–6). Abram believed God's promise but, as the years passed, his wife, Sarai, wasn't so sure. Did Sarai think God had forgotten His promise? Maybe she decided the Lord needed some help. For whatever reason, Sarai came up with a plan. She encouraged Abram to take her handmaiden, Hagar, into his bed. If God blessed Hagar with a son, Sarai would take the baby at birth and raise him as though he were her own.

Have you ever felt that God had forgotten a promise He made you? What happened when you tried to take matters into your own hands?

_____

_____

_____

_____

Really, it all comes down to a matter of faith and trust. Sarai didn't trust God to do what He had promised. She didn't have the faith to wait for God's timing. Why do we try to help God when He doesn't meet our expectations? When we try to "help" Him, it always backfires, doesn't it? As we follow the story of Sarai and Abram, we will see that the same thing happened to them.

Once Hagar was pregnant, tension arose between the two women. Should we be surprised? Hagar had something to flaunt in front of her mistress and Sarai became jealous and bitter. Finally Hagar ran away into the wilderness. Women had no value in ancient cultures so we can imagine the lack of concern over a missing handmaiden. No one was sent to look for her. No one was worried about whether she and her unborn child would die in the desert.

Hagar was inconsequential in the eyes of the world. But she was not inconsequential to the Lord of the universe. The same Lord who created the heavens and the earth, who knew each star by name, came personally to find Hagar. She didn't have to tell Him of the storm she was experiencing—God was already aware of the things Sarai had said and done to her. He calmed Hagar's fears and reassured her He would be with her and her unborn son for all their tomorrows. Hagar proclaimed, *"I have now seen the One who sees me"* (Genesis 16:13b).

Do you sometimes feel inconsequential in the eyes of the world around you? Do you wonder, "If I were to disappear, would anyone care?" Do you have any idea how very precious you are to God? Read the following verses and let them caress your heart. How does each one make you feel secure in God's love for you?

Do you have any idea how very precious you are to God?

"Let the beloved of the LORD rest secure in him, for he shields him all day long, and the one the LORD loves rests between his shoulders." (Deuteronomy 33:12)

_____

_____

_____

"You are forgiving and good, O LORD, abounding in love to all who call to you." (Psalm 86:5)

_____

_____

_____

"I have loved you with an everlasting love; I have drawn you with loving-kindness." (Jeremiah 31:3)

_____

_____

_____

"The LORD your God is with you, he is mighty to save. He will take great delight in you, he will quiet you with

_____

_____

Jesus is Trustworthy

DAY FIVE

his love, he will rejoice over you with singing." (Zephaniah 3:17)

_____

_____

"But when the kindness and love of God our Savior appeared, he saved us, not because of righteous things we had done, but because of his mercy." (Titus 3:4, 5a)

_____

_____

_____

_____

What a great love! Can you imagine your heavenly Father singing over you? When you clearly understand the love your heavenly Father has for you, you will trust Him to guide you.

DARING TO TRUST!

Do you find it hard to trust Jesus on the tough days? When I grow weary, I often keep pushing until I'm exhausted. I generally keep going, forgetting Jesus' promise that *"[my] yoke is easy and [my] burden is light"* (Matthew 11:30). When temptation comes, I tell myself I can resist it; I usually can't. Sometimes I close my eyes and hope it will be gone when I open them; it never is. I need to remember that Jesus understands my struggles and can guide me.

Trusting Jesus means we must surrender completely to Him and place our lives and the lives of those we love in His hands. It means we must follow Him as He leads us through the wind and the rain. Are we afraid He doesn't know the way? Are we afraid He's never handled anything as horrible as the storm we are facing? Why do our plans have to fail, leaving us stranded in the wild sea, before we realize we should've trusted Him from the beginning?

As Jesus traveled through His earthly life, He faced all the storms we will ever encounter—and more. Although we struggle with our weaknesses, we won't be crippled by them because Jesus overpowered each one. We can trust Him to heal our vulnerabilities and to give us the strength to walk in victory.

Although Satan tempts us over and over again, he won't attack us face-to-face, as he did Jesus in the wilderness. Because He disarmed every weapon in Satan's arsenal, Jesus can be trusted to guide us around the booby traps Satan sets for us. He frees us from the prison of our desires by leading us to God's Word, where our thirst is quenched. He satisfies our hunger for status and power by assuring us of eternal glory with Him.

When has God given you victory over weakness or temptation?

_____

_____

_____

Glory . . . Jesus came from heaven's glory to live an inglorious human existence. Why would He do that? Why would He endure the weaknesses of the human body? Why would He subject His holiness to Satan's temptation?

Listen to the words of Isaiah as he paints a picture of Jesus' true splendor: *"And he will be called Wonderful Counselor, Mighty God, Everlasting Father, Prince of Peace."* (Isaiah 9:6)

Why did the Wonderful Counselor choose to come to Earth to be surrounded by man's ungodly wisdom? Why would the mighty, everlasting Lord come to Earth clothed in the vulnerable, temporal body of a man? The Prince of Peace willingly endured ridicule, anger, and an unjust death. How amazing! Jesus did these things for us, to redeem us and make us the children of God.

APPLY Which characteristic of Jesus' glory is most important to you in your walk with Him?

_____

_____

_____

"He was despised and rejected by men, a man of sorrows, and familiar with suffering. . . . Surely he took up our infirmities and carried our sorrows." (Isaiah 53:3, 4)

". . . despised and rejected . . ." . . . From the very beginning of His ministry, Jesus was rejected by most everyone around Him. He offended the people of Israel because they expected their Messiah to come as a mighty king who would overthrow Rome and reestablish Israel's glory (Mark 15:18; John 6:15).

Merchants were angered because His miracles disrupted their business (Matthew 8:34). Yet others condemned Him to die because they accused Him of claiming to be king (Luke 23:2). He was rejected by those in his own hometown, and even by the disciples who fled when he was arrested and crucified (Matthew 26:56b; John 16:31, 32).

Jesus understands your heartache when you are rejected by those around you. When you don't meet the expectations of those around you and they react with anger, He understands. When you are ridiculed because you cling to your principles, Jesus sympathizes with your loneliness. Have you been chastised at work or even fired because you refused to go along with questionable practices? Jesus grieves with you. When your own family rejects you because of your faith in Him, Jesus identifies with your pain. You can trust Him to comfort you.

How has Jesus comforted you during a time of rejection?

_____

_____

_____

_____

". . . familiar with suffering . . ." Jesus experienced great physical and emotional suffering. Exhaustion: He was hounded continually by crowds who clamored for healing and miracles (Mark 3:20; John 6:1, 2). Aches: I'm sure

He had an aching back and feet from too many hours treading down hard, stony paths and too many nights spent sleeping on the ground with only a stone for a pillow—He didn't even have a home to call His own (Matthew 8:20). Sorrow: What deep sorrow He felt when He looked down on Jerusalem, His beloved city, and saw the masses who didn't believe in Him (Luke 13:34)!

No suffering that Jesus experienced during His ministry equaled the agony of the cross or the sorrow He endured during that dark time when the face of His Father turned away from Him (Matthew 27:45, 46). The holiness of His Father could not look upon the body of His Son, who carried the sins of all mankind (Habakkuk 1:13). What joy it must have been for Jesus to return to His Father and to be seated in glory at His right hand (Mark 16:19; Ephesians 1:20; Hebrews 2:9)!

We often tread through difficult days, perhaps dealing with a boss who wants us to perform "miracles" to complete a project in an unreasonably short period of time. It seems as if our husbands and kids pressure us continually to meet their needs. Jesus understands the strain that marks our days. How He grieves with us as we weep over a loved one who refuses to accept Jesus as Savior!

No matter the suffering we endure, we will never experience the agony of the cross. Praise God, Jesus took our suffering upon Himself! Never will we feel the total abandonment Jesus felt when His Father turned His face away. God promised to never leave us, to never forsake us. Even in our darkest hours, God will be there.

APPLY How does God's presence give you strength and courage when difficulty looms before you?

_____

_____

_____

_____

"Surely he took up our infirmities and carried our sorrows." How amazing that Jesus willingly set aside His glory as the everlasting King to humble Himself and take on the appearance of man (Daniel 7:13, 14; Philippians 2:6–11). He chose to be born in a cave, surrounded by animals, rather than to be born in a castle. He lived an itinerant lifestyle rather than live comfortably in a mansion. He accepted ridicule and rejection rather than receiving the praise he deserved as the Holy Son of God.

Strength instead of weakness; victory over sin . . . do these seem like impossibilities? We must remember that no path ahead of us is as horrific as was Jesus' path to the cross. Even though our course may be full of obstacles, it is already marked with Jesus' footsteps. And no sin is greater than God's power and forgiveness.

When has God given you victory in spite of your weaknesses?

_____

_____

God promised to never leave us, to never forsake us. Even in our darkest hours, God is there.

_____

_____

Jesus is worthy of our trust because He has walked where we walk. Jesus is worthy of our trust because He was willing to leave His heavenly throne and, as the perfect sacrificial Lamb, surrender His life. No one else loves us so completely! Jesus is worthy because His shed blood and His righteousness compose the solid foundation on which we stand when everything else is falling apart. With every step we take, God goes before us. The road has been prepared and our enemy has been conquered. Jesus walked before us, prevailing over every temptation, every fear, and every storm we face. We can hear His voice: "You have been delivered." We have been delivered from sin by His victory over Satan. We have been delivered from fear and uncertainty, from weakness to strength, because we can follow the footsteps of our great Shepherd who guides us.

The Lord, the Lord is our Rock! Even when the storm swirls around us, though our hearts may tremble, He pours out His love on us and holds us firmly in His hand. The road may be hard but we never walk it alone. When we see the storm clouds in the distance, when we feel the rain beating against our lives, even when we look back at the receding storm and wonder what God's purpose may have been through the pain . . . God is with us. Cling to Him!

Are you in a storm right now? If so, end this week by writing a prayer to God, asking Him to reveal Himself to you through the turmoil you are experiencing.

_____

_____

_____

_____

_____

_____

_____

_____

_____

_____

_____

_____

_____

_____

_____

_____

_____

_____

Notes

3

Life's Storms

Have you ever sat at your window and watched a storm roll in? At first, you see dark clouds off in the distance. Over the next few minutes, the clouds move closer and it becomes darker, as the sun is hidden. The wind picks up, carrying with it the sound of thunder. You hear the rain falling, gentle at first, and then a heavy downpour. Then as the drumming of the rain and the flashes of lightning begin to fade, the sun's rays reclaim the day.

Storms entering our lives often follow the same pattern. Something happens, perhaps a phone call or a medical diagnosis, and dark clouds that signal difficult days ahead appear on the horizon. Before long the storm hits; your worst fears come true in spite of your prayers. It seems as though the storm will never end. The harder the wind and rain pound your life, the deeper your doubt grows. Eventually, with hours on your knees before God and the prayers of Christian friends, you begin to trust God to guide you through. Finally the storm passes, leaving a life that will never be the same and a transformed relationship with God.

As we travel through this chapter, we'll examine the types of storms that disrupt our lives and we'll recognize the ways God reveals Himself through each one.

A STORM ARRAY

Storms come in every size, color, and flavor. Isn't it too bad they don't come in chocolate? The one thing all storms have in common is they disrupt our lives. Sometimes it's a rapid-fire series of small things that rob us of patience. Occasionally it's a catastrophe that tears up our lives and leaves permanent scars.

Our definition of a crisis changes as the years go by. What might've been a tragedy when we were younger seems minor compared with the storms we face today. When we were teenagers, we were devastated if our "one true love" left us for another girl. Now, if we face divorce, that past crisis seems trivial. As young mothers, toilet training seemed beyond our capability. Now that we're struggling to raise a teenager, we wish for those smaller battles. As young single women, we worry about an unexpected bill upending our tenuous one-salary finances. As we grow older and illness strikes, our single income is overwhelmed by medical bills that consume our savings and make our past worries seem so small in comparison. With wisdom, experience, and a closer walk with God, our perspective certainly changes.

What past storms seem like mere rain showers now? How or why has your perspective changed?

_____

_____

_____

_____

_____

Satan's attacks are tailor-made.

We each respond differently to the storms of life. Some of us are emotional; others remain calm. Some have the faith of Joseph (Genesis 37–50); others are bigger doubters than Thomas (John 20:19-25). How we respond isn't the most important thing. What's most critical is that we respond honestly. Our prayers should be an open conversation, expressing the depths of our hearts to God. Anger, frustration, pain, despair . . . all these can be brought to His throne. He'll never respond in anger to an honest expression of emotion. He'll submerge us in the depths of His love and heal our broken hearts.

We might marvel at the strength of a friend as she walks through a tragedy we know would destroy us. We might be shocked at the devastation of a loved one when the problem they face seems trivial to us. Satan's attacks are tailor-made. When the Enemy brings a storm into your life, he's careful to choose one that will impact you greatly. He doesn't care if it seems trivial to someone else, or even if it might've seemed trivial to you in the past. He only cares if it will upset your world right now. His goal is to destroy your faith and to defeat you. But remember—Jesus, your Shepherd, has measured the storm and He's found it worthy to enter your life. He's measured its refining effect: The wind's just strong enough to erode your weaknesses, the thunder's just loud enough to draw your eyes upward to God's face, and the driving rain's just hard enough to draw you closer to God's side, seeking shelter.

Storms in our lives take many forms. Most, if we'll admit it, are caused by our own foolish behavior. When we choose to disobey God, we can expect Him to discipline us, as any good father would. Occasionally, hardship comes with no reasonable explanation. Although the circumstances differ, our stormy experiences fall into one of the following categories:

- Common to every person: crises we share with everyone around us
- Consequences of personal sin: difficulties resulting from our own actions
- Consequences of another's sin: suffering caused by another's behavior
- Results of Satan's attack: the Enemy's attempt to disrupt our obedience to God

 Most of us have come through every type of struggle described above. What one time of suffering stands out in your mind?

_____

_____

_____

The cause of the crisis may vary, but when the wind rises and the downpour begins, the cause is unimportant to us. All we can think of is: When will this be over? We turn to God's Word and devour all the promises of deliverance we can find. We bargain with God and make all kinds of promises we can never keep, if He will just rescue us.

When deliverance doesn't come, we search for someone to blame. "All my friends were doing it so I thought it'd be okay." "If that doctor knew what he was doing, my best friend would still be alive." "If God loved me, He would've never allowed this to happen."

We seek any explanation we can to avoid accepting the truth of God's authority over our lives. Whether we like it or not, very moment is under His control—the good times and the bad (1 Samuel 2:6, 7). It's frightening to acknowledge that God allows suffering. "I don't deserve this, " we complain. "Nothing good can ever come out of this tragedy," we cry out. With these words we reject God's lordship in our lives. With these words we reject God's sovereignty.

How have you denied God's sovereignty during times of hardship?

_____

_____

_____

_____

Even though the storm rages, we find comfort in God's steady hand and unshakable character.

Our circumstances might change—God remains the same. Life might crumble around us—God is our Rock. Often, when the skies clear, we're able to see how He was working even in the hard times. God's never caught by surprise; His plans are already in place to guide us, teach us, and bring us through the storm. Take comfort in His presence!

Our circumstances might change—God remains the same.

The storms in our lives reveal God to us more fully.

We ask: How can the struggles we face be a part of God's plan? Yet, as we look back on difficult days, we recognize how much we learned about God. If we never know sorrow, we'll never know Him as Comforter. If we never know pain, we'll never know Him as Healer. If we never know need, we'll never know Him as Provider. The storms in our lives reveal God to us more fully.

How has God revealed Himself to you in past storms? What part of God's character do you need to minister to you in your current storm?

_____

_____

_____

_____

The storms of our lives are under His control. The rain only falls because God allows it. Suffering enters our lives only with God's approval. Satan only tempts us because God permits it. Through each difficult day, God's purpose is the thread that transforms the hours of chaos into a glorious pattern. He desires to move us from weakness to strength, from independence to total reliance on Him, from superficial faith to a deep walk with Him.

APPLY How has God transformed you through the hardships you've faced?

_____

_____

_____

_____

During this week we'll encounter men and women in Scripture who struggled with the same hardships we face. We'll see God work through each circumstance to teach and transform those people. By seeing the ways they respond, we'll learn how to walk with God through these same storms when they batter us.

Life's Storms

DAY TWO

COMMON STORMS

Sometimes we feel as if we're the only ones suffering, yet many crises are common to everyone—part of living and participating in the world. These range from catastrophes down to small irritations that pile up through the day. The sudden disaster, the unexpected bill, or the hole in our only pair of hose—these struggles enter into everyone's life, even though we might feel uniquely overwhelmed.

Natural disasters are the primary things we think about when considering storms we all have in common. For as long as we can remember, countless numbers all over the world have experienced the extremes nature can bring: droughts, floods, earthquakes, volcanic eruptions, tornadoes, and hurricanes. When we experience one of these firsthand, we can't complain, "Why is God doing this to ME?" The helicopter flying over the devastation shows that our suffering is common to everyone in our area.

Most of us might not encounter a natural disaster, but we all cope with much less dramatic crises. Repairs around the house, car repair, and children's illnesses are common to every one of us who lives in a house, drives a car, or has a child. We all experience these things—they're part of life.

For all of us, every new day brings a new challenge. New babies come; toddlers change to teenagers overnight. We become parents to our parents; we become parents to our grandchildren. Strain enters our marriages. Incomes grow tighter just as the cost of everything from food to clothes skyrockets. Even our bodies change: emotions, aches, and, oh, those power surges!

Describe a time when you felt like the only one who'd ever faced your problems.

_____

_____

_____

_____

After a hurricane devastated our area, everyone on my street ventured out to take inventory. Some homes looked as if they'd been attacked by an egg beater: roofs twisted, swing sets mangled, and trees leaning at odd angles. Amazingly, my house was still standing—minus three trees and a fence, but intact. Of course we were all without power, so our freezers and refrigerators were useless. We all gathered at the houses that had barbeque pits and a delicious smell settled over the neighborhood. We spent the next three weeks pooling all the food we had and eating our meals together. We encouraged each other, laughed together, and found a little sanity in the midst of the craziness.

Many stories in Scripture describe people struggling in the midst of disaster. One such story is found in Genesis 41. Famine was a continual fear in the land; it still is in many parts of the world. Joseph's actions during a famine can guide us as we face our hardships.

Joseph and the Famine
Joseph was a colorful character with a tumultuous life, recorded in Genesis 37–50. A brash and conceited young man, his brothers sold him into slavery in Egypt. Now that's sibling rivalry taken to a whole new level! In Egypt, he was falsely accused of rape and imprisoned. After several years, Pharaoh called on him to interpret a perplexing dream: Seven fat cows were devoured by seven starving cows. God revealed to Joseph the meaning of the dream: Seven years of riches and plenty would be followed by seven years of severe famine. To reward Joseph's wisdom, Pharaoh released him from prison and placed him in control over all Egypt.

Be Prepared
Joseph immediately began to prepare for the coming famine (Genesis 41:47–49). During the seven years of abundance, he ordered each city to save the excess grain in great storehouses. So much grain was stored that no one could even keep track of the amount. Because of this preparation, Egypt had plenty of grain to feed its people when the famine struck.

Many problems we experience happen to everyone— they're part of life.

We must trust God to guide us before, during, and after the storm.

That's fine for Joseph, but how do we prepare for the sudden adversity that enters our lives? Many disasters seem to come out of nowhere. But very few difficulties hit without any warning signs. If we're alert, we can weather the storms.

How can we be ready when a monster tornado plunges down from a violent sky? When I was young, we lived in an area famous for frequent tornadoes. Whenever severe weather would roll in, my parents would corral us kids and we'd huddle in a small inner closet, with a game for diversion and our battery-powered radio. Being watchful during severe weather and having a defined plan to follow at a moment's notice saved our family's lives. Oh—and we always made sure our homeowners insurance was paid up-to-date!

How can we be prepared when a financial crisis devastates our lives? My husband and I have struggled through the years to set aside a few dollars each month into an emergency fund. We drew on our savings many times to cover an unexpected bill. Was it always enough? No, but it did prevent a crisis from becoming a disaster.

There are many ways we can be prepared for the unexpected: family fire drills, money for a rainy day, and friends we can trust to meet our needs in difficult times. Being prepared doesn't always avert disaster but it can aid us in rebuilding our lives. Above all, we must trust God to guide us before, during, and after the storm.

When have you faced a crisis that was or could've been avoided (or at least alleviated) by being prepared?

_____

_____

_____

_____

Share with Others

Reaching out to others brings beauty out of tragedy.

When the famine hit, how did Joseph respond? He could've seized all the grain to ensure that the powerful in Egypt were well fed and left the masses to fend for themselves. Isn't that what politicians usually do? Instead, he opened the storehouses to the starving people in the region. Joseph's willingness to share with others saved many from starvation (Genesis 41:53–57).

When disaster hits, we're often so focused on our own problems we forget to consider the plight of others around us. Some might've suffered an even greater loss than we have. Many are in more dire economic situations than we are. Looking at the impact of the storm on others allows us to recognize the blessings God has heaped upon us. Reaching out to others brings beauty out of tragedy.

When a dear elderly woman in my church was financially crippled by a car repair bill, her Sunday School class decided to take up a collection for a "member in need." As the hat was passed, this sweet woman dug around in her purse and brought out a few coins to add to the collection. Those who knew of her situation felt their eyes fill with tears. She had every right to let the hat pass by but her heart desired to give to another suffering soul. As you can imagine, when the collection was presented to her, there wasn't a dry eye in the place! When hardship invades my life, I find myself asking: Is my heart filled with compassion, or with selfishness?

Has your region been devastated by an occurrence of nature's violence? Are there others around you who've lost much more than you have? Perhaps you can reach out and help them with a warm blanket or a few children's clothes. Has an unexpected bill strained your finances? Perhaps you can still donate a few items to the food pantry to help those facing greater hardship. Our gratitude to God for His provision in times of hardship should spill out through our actions.

APPLY When have you set aside your own problems to help someone impacted worse than you?

_____

_____

_____

Cry for Help

The situation became desperate as the famine spread throughout the region. Families faced starvation as crops withered and livestock died. Rather than huddle in their homes in pride, they came to Joseph for food (Genesis 41:57). They knew of Joseph's supply and trusted him to meet their needs.

Why do we find it so hard to be open about our needs? Are we afraid of being ridiculed? Perhaps we're embarrassed because we feel like failures. Times of need enter everyone's life and God usually chooses to demonstrate His provision through the hearts and hands of those around us. We shouldn't sit home and wait for God to meet our needs in some miraculous way. When we refuse to ask for help, we rob others of God's blessing.

Several years ago, a friend experienced a staggering loss. She came to our pastor and described her situation and the provision she would need. The next Sunday morning service, one of our deacons simply said a member was in trouble and needed help. When the money collected that morning was counted, the amount was within a dollar of what the young lady needed. Imagine our joy, even tears, to recognize the way God had used each one of us, no matter the size of our gifts. If this young lady had hidden her need, we would have missed a great blessing. God's command to bear one another's burdens can only be obeyed when we're willing to share our burdens.

Why have you resisted sharing your needs with others?

_____

_____

_____

_____

_____

God usually chooses to demonstrate His provision through the hearts and hands of those around us.

Every choice we make should be measured against the standard of God's Word.

CONSEQUENCES OF OUR SIN

Natural disasters make headlines every day, but an overwhelming number of our hardships are caused by our own poor choices. Sin is the most destructive force in our lives. As we look around our world today, we see the devastating consequences of sin. God's standards are ignored by most societies, including our own.

Not only does the world suffer the consequences of sin, but our trials are often the logical consequences of our own sinful actions and choices. Generally, we'd rather blame someone or something else for our misfortunes than take responsibility for our own actions: "If my husband met my needs, I wouldn't turn to my co-worker." "If my professor explained things better, I wouldn't need to cheat on my tests."

If we're honest, we'll admit that most of our difficulties are the end result of our own sin. Many of our sins lead to "minor" consequences, while others have life-changing effects.

What difficult consequences do you see as you look at the sin in our society, or perhaps at a sinful choice you've made?

_____

_____

_____

Sin is disobedience to God; it begins in our thoughts, dictates our attitudes, and pours out through our words and actions. Certainly a "little white lie" now and then doesn't hurt anything, right? But eventually dishonesty becomes easier and easier, and we lose the trust of those we love. When we allow our minds to be filled with society's views on sex, promiscuous behavior is easy to justify.

When we make these choices, are we considering the cost? Usually not—we focus on the pleasure we expect to experience. We're masters of rationalization, aren't we? We make the wrong seem so right! We soothe our consciences with the argument that our behavior's acceptable in our society. After all, we argue, the world's different now. Surely God's laws don't apply any more.

APPLY How have you rationalized your choices in the past, even though you knew you were disobeying God? What have the consequences taught you about God?

_____

_____

_____

_____

God's standards haven't changed, even though society has. When we look around us, behavior that was wrong yesterday is accepted today. Trying to live our lives by society's morality is like trying to tread water in quicksand. The consistency of God's laws provides the lifeline we can hold on to when the lines between right and wrong begin to blur. Every choice we make should be measured against the standard of God's Word.

All of us have lost our footing and slid into sin. As any loving Father, God doesn't ignore our behavior; He holds us accountable for our actions. Because of His love He requires His children to obey the family rules, and disciplines us when we misbehave.

Even in our disobedience, God will never leave us or reject us. Rejoice in this: His love for you never changes—no matter your mistake. Jesus' death covers all sin and God is faithful to forgive when we confess our sin and ask for His strength to change our behavior (1 John 1:9).

Naive Eve

Sin and consequences have been roommates since the first couple was created. The lies Satan tells us in order to trick us into sin haven't changed, either. If we examine Eve's encounter with the serpent, we'll become aware of Satan's tactics.

> Now the serpent was more crafty than any of the wild animals the LORD God had made. He said to the woman, "Did God really say, 'You must not eat from any tree in the garden'?" The woman said to the serpent, "We may eat fruit from the trees in the garden, but God did say, 'You must not eat fruit from the tree that is in the middle of the garden ,and you must not touch it, or you will die.'" "You will not surely die," the serpent said to the woman. "For God knows that when you eat of it your eyes will be opened, and you will be like God, knowing good and evil." When the woman saw that the fruit of the tree was good for food and pleasing to the eye, and also desirable for gaining wisdom, she took some and ate it. (Genesis 3:1–6)

Satan's first objective was to cast doubt on God's Word. "Did God really say that?" If he could make Eve doubt God's commandment, she'd be defenseless against his scheme. Satan bombards us with the same argument every day, in a more subtle way. He tries to convince us God doesn't really mean what He says or that it no longer applies to us. After all, thousands of years have passed! How often do we fall for Satan's "times have changed" argument?

As soon as we begin to question God's Word, we let our guard down and we're on the road to disaster. If we doubt God's standards in one area, our beliefs in the others fall one by one like autumn leaves. Gossip, dishonesty, or immorality becomes easy because the question has taken up residence in our minds: Did God really say that?

When has Satan caused you to question the truth of God's commands?

_____

_____

_____

_____

We can protect ourselves from Satan's lies by knowing God's Word.

We can protect ourselves from Satan's lies by knowing God's Word. Nothing is more powerful than God's Word as our shield against doubt (Psalm 119:11). But we must put His words into action. Although Eve quoted God's words right back at Satan, that wasn't enough—she stayed to listen to more. If she'd clung to the truth and walked away, the fruit would still be hanging on the tree! When we find ourselves in a tempting situation, God's Word comes into our minds and warns us to walk away. Yet we stay, mesmerized by the forbidden fruit. It's dangerous to flirt with sin. We may think we can resist it but it will draw us in if we stay within its reach. God gives us the escape route: His Word. Do we take it?

When have you faced temptation and listened to Satan's voice rather than God's warnings?

_____

_____

_____

Now that Satan had Eve in his grasp, he took it another step. *"You will not surely die."* He called God a liar! He told Eve there would be no consequences for her actions. This lie is rampant today. Common entertainment depicts a world where sinful behavior is rewarded with status and happiness. When we dabble in sin and nothing happens, we feel safe to wade in deeper. But defying God's Word is dangerous—what He says, He means.

God is faithful to guide us away from sin but we have to take His hand.

All of us are eager to learn His promises and we cling to them for comfort when we face difficulties. But it's just as important to know His warnings and to heed the consequences He describes. Listen to that small voice that warns you, "Don't do that—you'll be sorry if you do!" God is faithful to guide us away from sin but we have to take His hand.

Satan's last lie was, and still is, the most attractive of all: *"You will be like God."* Eve's mind was captivated by the idea she could be God. She could decide right from wrong. She could determine her own fate. How intoxicating that idea is, even today. We want to make our own decisions, apart from God's Word. We want to define sin to suit ourselves. We claim we know as much as God and we want to command our own future.

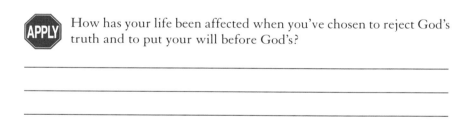 How has your life been affected when you've chosen to reject God's truth and to put your will before God's?

_____

_____

_____

_____

The surest way to prove the wisdom of God's leadership is to look back at some of our disastrous decisions. When we try to take life into our own hands, it invariably leads to a mess. When will we learn? God is God, we are not (Psalm 100:3)! Selfishness leads to sorrow. Only God knows the way leading to joy and victory.

Listening to Satan always leads to disastrous consequences, as it did for Eve. Before her sin, she enjoyed the continual presence of God. Afterward, she faced separation from Him. Her eternal life in the beautiful garden was replaced by life in a cold world—and she faced death.

Although we always face consequences, they aren't limited to our circumstances. The most disastrous consequence for Eve—and for us today—is separation from God. As His children, our eternal life with God can never be lost, but sin disrupts our daily relationship with Him. Time with God feels uncomfortable, so our prayers become superficial. Every sermon we hear in church seems aimed straight at us. Peace is replaced by a nagging guilt. God will fill our minds with turmoil until we admit our sin and ask for forgiveness. Immediately the barrier dissolves and our peace is restored.

Eve was no match for the evil serpent and neither are we. Even though we're armed with God's weapons, we don't put up much of a fight when Satan tempts us. Just like Eve, we'll incur the consequences, consequences that may scar our lives forever. We must run from temptation, cling to God's truth, and surrender to Him. Only then will we grow in obedience and experience the fullness of God's presence.

LIFE ISN'T FAIR

Although it's hard to deal with suffering caused by our own sin, at least we can understand the justice of reaping what we sow. However, when we're innocent victims, the pain's more difficult to bear. Most often, someone, perhaps someone we don't even know, makes a poor choice and the consequences pound our lives like waves on the shore. What's going on? What can God accomplish in our hearts and lives when we're blindsided through no fault of our own?

Occasionally, when we've determined to obey God, Satan sets out to run our lives through a meat grinder. Why would God call us to do something and then stand by while Satan wrecks our lives? What can God possibly hope to accomplish when our hearts are too broken to carry on?

When we're caught in these situations, we tend to cry out to God, "It's not fair!" You're right—it isn't fair. God is not interested in fairness; He's interested in molding us into the image of His Son. But how can He mold a shattered life? No matter the circumstance, God can teach us. Living through the consequences of another's sin will remove any shred of self-sufficiency, cause us to cling to Him and—most importantly—teach us to forgive when it's hardest. Being battered by Satan will erase any pride and self-righteousness we may feel and prove to us that, without God, we can accomplish nothing. Life isn't fair; it's a difficult process used by God to replace a character weakness with a strength and to teach us something about Himself.

Consequences of Another's Sin
Occasionally we're innocent bystanders, caught up in the tragic drama being played out around us. Perhaps we're in an accident caused by a drunk driver. Maybe one of us is dealing with the emotional and physical suffering from past abuse. Perhaps we have an officemate with a terrible temper—and we're often caught in the explosion.

It seems so senseless. We hurl angry questions at God or demand He attack the person responsible for our pain. When my life was torn apart by malicious

God is not interested in fairness; He's interested in molding us into the image of His Son.

lies, I admit I relished the thought of watching God destroy the person responsible. God chose not to teach me of vengeance; He chose to stretch my faith and teach me that His grace is sufficient.

APPLY How has God deepened your faith when you've suffered because of another person's sin?

_____

_____

_____

Down through the ages, God's people have endured suffering because of another's sin. We've already seen the hardship in David's life caused by the sinful jealousy of King Saul. Now let's meet Leah, a young woman sacrificed on the altar of greed by her father, Laban (Genesis 29ff).

Leah's Despair
Leah was a young woman living in her father's household. Her sister, Rachel, was a beautiful girl; Leah wasn't so blessed. It already seems unfair, doesn't it?

Along came Jacob, seeking asylum in Laban's household. He'd fled for his life from his own family because he'd cheated to gain his brother's portion of the family inheritance. An interesting cast of characters: Jacob, Leah, and Rachel—along with Laban, who decided to take advantage of the situation.

True to any good story, Jacob and Rachel fell hopelessly in love. When Jacob asked for Laban's blessing, Laban saw an opportunity to profit from the situation. He demanded that Jacob work for him for seven years. Jacob's wage was Rachel's hand in marriage—paid at the end of the seven years. After that, Jacob and Rachel could return to Jacob's homeland and set up their own household.

As time passed, Jacob's work made Laban a very prosperous man and he devised a plan to keep Jacob from leaving. At the wedding, Laban substituted Leah for Rachel. Jacob didn't realize what had happened until it was too late. As you can imagine, he was furious. He didn't care about Leah—he loved Rachel. In his greed, Laban insisted that Jacob work another seven years before he could marry Rachel. Love-struck, Jacob agreed.

Can you imagine how Leah felt as this story unfolded? Her father forced her to marry a man who didn't love her (and vice versa, very possibly). Did she grieve, knowing her father didn't love her as much as he loved prosperity? Did her heart break as she listened to Jacob loudly insist he didn't want her and would never love her?

Leah suffered because of her father's sinful greed and because of Jacob's self-centered cruelty. Jacob didn't care about Leah's sorrow; he showed her no love and kindness. In fact, when Leah gave birth to Jacob's first son, her cry was, _"Surely my husband will love me now"_ (Genesis 29:32). It's hard to imagine Leah's heartache. She was tortured by the sins of those she loved.

Many of us have lived through this kind of agony. Perhaps a co-worker stepped all over you to get that promotion. Have you been devastated by the obvious favoritism your parents showed a sibling? Has your sense of safety been dashed by the deliberate choice someone made to rob your home?

How should we respond when the sinfulness of others brings pain into our lives? Let's learn from Leah. Over and over, Scripture records her prayers. She may not have understood the horror she experienced but she understood this: God was listening to her and He would answer her prayers. God drew near to her and enabled Leah to find happiness through her many sons.

This is our only comfort: God hears our prayers. He'll draw near to us to provide strength and comfort. He'll wash away the bitterness and anger and teach us to forgive. He'll bring us honor as others watch the way we respond. Our circumstances may not change but God will heal us and restore our joy.

How has God brought healing into your life when you've suffered because of another's sinful choices?

Remarkably, Leah never seemed to lash out at Jacob and seek to destroy him. Instead, she willingly submitted to a physical relationship with him even though she knew he didn't love her. In the same way, God asks us to love and forgive those who harm us. God alone heals bitterness and erases the desire to retaliate. He alone enables us to respond to those people with love and kindness.

Difficulties Due to Satan's Attack

It's always more satisfying to blame our hardships on Satan than take the responsibility for our own sin. It's especially gratifying to give him credit for undeserved suffering. In truth, Satan's attacks are rare and there are several distinct characteristics that signal his destructive work. His desire is that we doubt God's love, His sovereignty, and His power.

First, Satan's assault comes at us from every direction. The car breaks down, family stress builds, problems surface at work—every facet of our life is affected, seemingly without a reason. Satan's goal is to cause us to doubt God's love and protection. How can God allow our lives to disintegrate like this?

Another key mark of Satan's work is timing. Disaster spirals out of control and hardship piles upon hardship. If illness strikes your family, a huge unexpected bill surfaces, and a difficult co-worker goes on a rampage—all in just a few days—then you can be sure it's Satan's handiwork. His purpose in the attack is to cause you to doubt God's sovereignty. Where's God's power? Why isn't He able to stop all this? Is He really in control?

The most telling characteristic is the crumbling of our lives just after we've made a commitment to God. Have you committed to spend time with God every morning? In every way imaginable, your mornings will be disrupted.

Our circumstances might not change but God will heal us and restore our joy.

Have you answered God's call to serve in your church? Expect your life to disintegrate around you. Satan will rob you of your time and energy until serving God seems impossible. Satan's goal is to frustrate and defeat you. "Is this what I get for following God's will?" you ask. "Well, it isn't worth it!"

APPLY Can you identify a time when a commitment to God was followed by one hardship after another?

_____

_____

_____

_____

A few months after I lost my job, I felt God's calling to write this study. But I was an engineer—engineers write technical manuals, not Bible studies! After much encouragement from my husband and close Christian friends, I agreed to give it a try. Several months later, I heard about a writers conference. Although I thought we couldn't afford for me to go, my husband insisted, so off I went. God used that conference to confirm His call and to encourage me to believe in His enabling.

What do you think happened when I returned home? Within days, I became very ill. The sewer line in our backyard had to be replaced, a hailstorm destroyed our roof, and both cars broke down. Coincidence? I don't think so! I'd made a commitment to God and Satan was angry. He threw everything at me to break my resolve and to destroy my confidence in God. At first I was angry and devastated. I gave up and began to hunt for a "real" job. But friends and loved ones prayed for me and encouraged me. Slowly God opened my eyes to Satan's plan and strengthened my determination to be obedient.

How have you responded when Satan's attack was obvious?

_____

_____

_____

Poor Paul

The most striking example we find in Scripture of Satan's attack is the life of the apostle Paul. God transformed Paul's life and called him to be a witness to the Gentiles. Paul surrendered to God's call and spent the rest of his life proclaiming the gospel throughout the Roman Empire. God worked miracles through Paul—and thousands became Christians.

How do you think Satan responded to Paul's commitment and service? He went on a rampage! Paul was imprisoned many times, beaten until near death, shipwrecked, attacked mercilessly by the Jews, stoned . . . the list goes on and on.

How did Paul respond? If he'd given up, you and I wouldn't be Christians today! Instead, he told his jailers about Jesus, he kept witnessing in the face of persecution, and he praised God for the opportunity to suffer for Him. What was Satan's intention? To attack Paul so severely he would call it quits. But with every blow, Paul's dependence on God grew, his faith matured, and his determination increased. Satan made a grave error: He underestimated God's power and Paul's stubbornness. Am I like Paul? Probably not. I would've given up!

Satan knows exactly how to attack each of us to achieve his goals. The question is: Why does God allow him to badger us? Does He need to find out how we respond? No, He already knows that. Then, why? He wants us to examine our hearts and discover the level of our commitment. He wants to teach us we're completely dependent on Him and that we can only accomplish His will through His power. He wants to fill us with the joy of victory.

When have you stayed the course, in spite of Satan's attack?

_____

_____

_____

_____

> *We are completely dependent on God and we can only accomplish His will through His power.*

QUIETING THE STORM

Sometimes I look around me and I just wish for some peace and quiet. Have you ever wanted to step out of your life and let someone else deal with it for a while? When life becomes too much to bear, my favorite fantasy is about driving to a nearby hotel and checking in without telling anyone where I've gone. I blissfully ignore all the turmoil in my life. I turn on the TV, only to see my family and the police looking frantically for me. At some point I'll let them know where I am, but for now I just want to be left alone.

Of course I've never acted on my crazy notion; we shouldn't just walk away from life. Disasters strike our neighborhoods, the fallout from some stupid act turns things upside down—storms come into our lives.

Do you occasionally feel as if God has retreated and left you to handle things on your own? As if He has gone to the French Riviera for a vacation? The disciples would understand that feeling. They panicked in the face of storms, just as we do. They cried out to Jesus, just as we do. The story of Jesus' response to them will teach us how He works in our circumstances today.

A Stormy Sea

> *"That day when evening came, he said to his disciples, "Let us go over to the other side." Leaving the crowd behind, they took him along, just as he was, in the boat. There were also other boats with him."* (Mark 4:35, 36)

Jesus and the disciples spent the day at Peter's house. Jesus had healed everyone who came to Him and He was exhausted. He and the disciples set off on a small boat across the Sea of Galilee to escape the crowds. I'm sure the disciples chattered excitedly about the miracles they'd seen Jesus perform.

Perhaps they marveled at His power and felt sure nothing could harm them while in His presence.

It's easy to have faith during the good times. It's easy to become excited and feel free from danger when we've recently watched Him work in our lives. When life's good, we give no thought to tomorrow. But when the storms arise, our faith isn't so strong.

> *"A furious squall came up, and the waves broke over the boat, so that it was nearly swamped. Jesus was in the stern, sleeping on a cushion."* (Mark 4:37, 38a)

Soon after the boat left the shore, a storm exploded and the waves began to crash over the boat. Of course, the disciples panicked, just as we do when a storm erupts up in our lives. Jesus was asleep in the back of the boat. Isn't it amazing that Jesus was calm enough to take a nap? Jesus knew the storm was only momentary. He trusted His Father to protect Him, even while the boat churned.

Sleep . . . How precious sleep is when our minds are spinning due to the storms swirling around us! Somehow misery is magnified in the dark. Trusting God is harder to do at midnight than at noon. If we fill our minds with the words of God, peace will silence the thoughts that torture our minds. When I experience sleepless nights, I turn to a set of Scripture passages I keep on a card in the drawer by my bed.

Jesus knows the nature of our storms. He sees the beginning and the end. We should trust Him enough to rely on Him to guide us through the storm. No matter the intensity, remember—Jesus is in the storm.

📖 Read the Scriptures below and describe how they give rest to your mind and allow you to sleep.

> *"Let the beloved of the* Lord *rest secure in him, for he shields him all day long, and the one the* Lord *loves rests between his shoulders."* (Deuteronomy 33:12)

> *"My Presence will go with you, and I will give you rest."* (Exodus 33:14)

> *"I lie down and sleep; I wake again, because the* Lord *sustains me."* (Psalm 3:5)

> *"I will lie down and sleep in peace, for you alone, O* Lord*, make me dwell in safety."* (Psalm 4:8)

> *"When you lie down, you will not be afraid; when you lie down, your sleep will be sweet."* (Proverbs 3:24)

How do the Scripture verses above give rest to your mind and allow you to sleep?

_____

_____

_____

_____

_____

No matter the intensity, remember—Jesus is in the storm.

"The disciples woke him and said to him, 'Teacher, don't you care if we drown?' He got up, rebuked the wind and said to the waves, 'Quiet! Be still!' Then the wind died down and it was completely calm." (Mark 4:38b, 39)

As the storm intensified, the disciples shook Jesus and cried out, *"Teacher, don't you care if we drown?"* Don't You care? . . . How often I've said that to Him. "Don't You care if I drown in assignments at work?" "Don't You care if I'm overwhelmed by the continual demands of my toddler?" "Don't You care if my finances are a wreck?" Why do I use the turmoil in my day as a measure of His love for me?

When have you told God He didn't care? How did He assure you of His concern for you?

_____

_____

_____

_____

God cares for us and He's watchful every minute of every one of our days. He never takes His eyes off us and He never neglects us (Psalm 34:15).

When Jesus heard the cry of the disciples, He immediately rebuked the storm and all became quiet. Don't you wish He'd stand in the midst of your storm and silence it? Often He doesn't choose to do that, but He can calm the whirlwind in your heart and mind. Only Jesus can bring peace as the storm rages. Only Jesus can keep your feet on the Solid Rock when everything is shifting under your feet.

> *"He said to his disciples, 'Why are you so afraid? Do you still have no faith?' They were terrified and asked each other, 'Who is this? Even the wind and the waves obey him!'"* (Mark 4:40–41)

"Why are you so afraid?" Jesus whispers that question to our hearts when we cower in fear. As we look back to the storms we've experienced in the past, we remember His presence and His guidance. Yet we so easily give in to fear. We so easily lose our faith. The Holy Spirit is within us and God surrounds us. We can be assured of His watch-care over us. He promised to never leave us or forsake us (Joshua 1:5). We can trust God's presence and His vigil over us.

 When the disciples saw how the wind and waves obeyed Jesus' voice, they were amazed and terrified. When were you last amazed at His sovereign work in your life? When have you been in awe of God's power over your circumstances?

_____

_____

_____

_____

Even during our crises, God's power is evident in His actions as He directs each detail of our difficult days. The wind and waves that assault our lives are continuously under His control.

Only Jesus can keep your feet on the Solid Rock when everything is shifting under your feet.

A life with no storms is a life that enjoys no deepening intimacy with God.

While the storm raged, the disciples' faith buckled. Then, when they saw Jesus' power over the storm, they were amazed and recognized Him as the Son of God. Trust came easy to them on the good days but fear overcame them when a crisis hit. Sound familiar?

Our paths are traveled in both sunshine and rain; our Lord desires us to trust Him, no matter our circumstances. In this study, I use the analogy of a storm to describe the impact of a crisis on our lives and on our faith because I often exclaim, "Lord, I love the fresh smell of the earth after the rain!" How my silly heart wants freshness in my life without experiencing storms. How I want to rejoice in mountaintop experiences without walking through the valleys separating them. Yet I know that a life with no storms and no valleys is a life that remains flat and barren like the desert—a life that enjoys no deepening intimacy with God.

When the storm strikes, we often respond with fear, confusion, even panic. How can Jesus understand our circumstances? As we study Jesus' life, we discover that He faced every storm we face: temptation, disappointment, and ridicule. God can and will use each trial to bring His glory and His victory into our lives—if we trust Him.

APPLY How have you seen Jesus use a trial or difficulty to bring His glory and victory into your life?

_____

_____

_____

_____

_____

_____

Are you ready to step into the storm? Over the next few weeks, you'll learn from men and women in Scripture who saw the storm coming and responded as it moved through their lives. Even though they stammered and stumbled, they all clung to God as He carried them through the downpour.

Notes

Notes

4

Dark Clouds Gather

We all have bad days, don't we? Occassionaly, everything seems to go wrong. The kids get into a huge fight at breakfast and the rest of the day is downhill from there. Or the phone rings just as you're heading out the door—starting the morning in a rush puts the whole day out of sorts. But we muddle through because we know tomorrow's a new day.

There are times when difficult days line up like a trail of ants making their way across the floor. You drive home from work, convinced this will be a peaceful evening with your husband—you've been fighting a lot lately. Or you sit on the couch, watching the sunrise, and you just know today will be the day you get a job offer that turns your life around. The days might be hard but you're filled with hope for tomorrow.

But then, your hopes fade as storm clouds gather in the distance and cast a shadow over your day. They might be the huge, black thunderheads of a severe storm or the smaller, gray clouds that bring a ground-soaking rain; it doesn't matter. They're storm clouds and they're headed your way! The normal day you were enjoying is suddenly twisted by the apprehension of what might happen. You're paralyzed by "what ifs." You call your friends and cry out, "What am I going to do?" You ask them to pray for you, and if you can calm down enough, you pray for yourself.

Many storms moved through Jesus' life but none was so severe as the dark cloud of the cross. Certainly He was aware of His destiny throughout His ministry, but in the last few weeks of His life, the storm clouds crept closer. How did He deal with the fear and the desire to flee that, in His humanness, He surely felt? He depended upon His Father! Let's turn to the greatest Teacher of all to see how He handled a day when storm clouds filled His horizon. I know I can learn much from sitting at His feet. How about you?

DARKNESS ON THE HORIZON

The clouds that threaten our lives come in every size and severity.

The phone rings. Remember your doctor's appointment last week? You feel fine, but you hear a voice say that the results are abnormal and more tests need to be done.

Your husband calls: Because of changes in the economy the company is considering layoffs; affected employees will be notified in two weeks.

Oh, it's your boss on the line—he wants you to work closely with *her* on this new project. "Lord, I don't know what it is about her but she just gets all over my last nerve in two minutes! How can I keep my cool over these next two months? You have to help me!"

Perhaps a family member calls to tell you there's been a car wreck and a loved one is in serious condition. "Can you come?" they ask.

Great, the school's calling. Your child can't seem to behave in the classroom and is waiting for you in the principal's office . . . again. But you have a mandatory staff meeting in thirty minutes. Life would be so much easier if you weren't a single parent.

You spilled your coffee this morning . . . the pair of slacks you'd like to wear won't zip . . . it took you forever to find your keys . . . and now the car needs gas—is it going to be one of those days?

How do you react when you see storm clouds moving into your life? Do you pray, and, if so, how?

_____

_____

_____

I must admit, I feel very free telling God exactly what I'd like Him to do in every situation. Ephesians 6:18 tells us to pray every day about everything, and I take that to heart. When I'm aware of storm clouds looming in the distance, I'm very specific: I want them gone, and I want them gone *now*. Immediately after I utter this "pious" prayer, I leap up and run over to the window to see if they're still there! Is it wrong to ask God to take the storm clouds away? How should we respond when we see storm clouds gathering on the horizon and know that tomorrow will be a rough day if we don't take action?

Jesus' early years allowed us to see Him in a new way: as our High Priest, who fully understands our joys and our sorrows. During the three years of His ministry, He revealed the Father to those with whom He walked, and to us, through the words recorded about His life. As we watched Jesus show compassion, wisdom, and power, we saw God. In His last few days, a storm hovered on the horizon and Jesus had to walk this path—not only as God, but also as man. Although we must never forget Jesus is fully God, there's so much we can learn from Him if we allow Him to teach us through His humanness.

Perhaps it was easy for Jesus to ignore the dark horizon as He rode into Jerusalem the Sunday before Passover. He could've chosen to ride into the city on a proud steed with sword raised—instead He chose to make His way through the streets on a lowly donkey (Matthew 21:4–7).

As Jesus and His disciples traveled to Jerusalem, they would have been engulfed by a large crowd of pilgrims on their way into the city to celebrate Passover (John 12:12). As Jesus neared the gate of the city, He found Himself surrounded by adoring crowds (John 12:13). The custom of the day was to greet a victorious king by throwing cloaks on the ground before him. As the people surrounded Him, they spread their cloaks and palm branches on the highway leading into Jerusalem from the Mount of Olives (Matthew 21:8). In their minds He was not a lowly Savior—He was the king who would deliver them from Roman oppression.

The crowds shouted "Hosanna!"—"Save us, help us!" They exalted Him as the "Son of David," a term from the Old Testament used to describe the Messiah (Matthew 21:9). Although Zechariah describes the king of Israel as humble (Zechariah 9:9), the people envisioned Jesus as a military conqueror. Their cries for salvation expressed their desire to see Jesus overthrow the Roman rule and restore Israel to its former glory.

Their desire for deliverance blinded them to Jesus' true identity. They praised Him as One who "came in the name of the Lord." Jesus didn't come in the name of the Lord—He came as the Lord! Even though they cried out in joyous excitement, they refused to see Jesus as the Lamb of God who came to take away the sins of the world (John 1:29).

When has your desire to be rescued blinded you to the glory and sovereignty of God?

_____

_____

_____

How often are our eyes so focused on the deliverance we desire from God that we miss His presence?

How often are our eyes so focused on the deliverance we desire from God that we miss His presence? We praise Him and exalt Him, not as Lord and Savior but as the One who'll rescue us. When He allows the storm clouds to continue their march into our lives, do we turn to Him in disbelief and ask, "Who are you?" much as the people inside Jerusalem did (Matthew 21:10)?

We often wish to make Jesus into the image we want—a powerful protector—rather than accept His will for our lives.

I'm sure Satan tempted Jesus again to claim His victory and glory without enduring the cross. He could claim His throne as king, surrounded by His adoring subjects. He could restore His beloved Jerusalem to power and glory. He could be the military Savior of Israel without becoming the spiritual Savior of all mankind. How delicious that must've seemed: to taste glory rather than agony. But Jesus stayed on the path ordained for Him—because He focused on a greater glory (Hebrews 12:2).

Even now, among the shouts of praise, the first wisp of clouds appeared on the horizon. When the chief priests and the scribes heard the people and watched the things Jesus did, they became angry. Already the seeds of a murderous plot had sprouted in their minds.

Could Jesus see the dark clouds of hatred coming into view? Could He feel the cold wind of rejection and false accusations? As Jesus saw His darkest days hovering on the horizon, He reacted in much the same way we might: He turned to His dear friends and cried out to His Father. Let's follow Him as He approaches the Garden of Gethsemane.

Dark Clouds
Gather

DAY TWO

A PRECIOUS PASSOVER

"And He said to them, 'I have eagerly desired to eat this Passover with you before I suffer. For I tell you, I will not eat it again until it finds fulfillment in the kingdom of God.'" (Luke 22:15, 16)

Passover is such a beautiful feast—a glorious celebration of God's love for and protection of His people Israel, demonstrated in Egypt so many centuries before (Exodus 11–12). God covered His people with His powerful hand and protected them from death as it swept through Egypt. Yet this feast had a deeper meaning. It was a picture of God's mercy and saving grace, which would be extended to all mankind through the death and resurrection of Jesus Christ. Just as the blood of a lamb protected His people from death so many centuries ago (Exodus 12:7, 13), the death of Jesus would cover us with His blood and rescue us from the power of death—forever (Hebrews 9:14).

How precious the Passover celebration must have been to Jesus that night! And yet, in some ways, it was a two-edged sword. It brought into even sharper view the terrible path lying before Him. To offer forgiveness of sin, along with deliverance from death to eternal life, Jesus had to endure suffering and death. Only through His agony could we be saved. As Jesus celebrated the truth of God's deep love and care for His own, how it must've calmed His troubled spirit.

 Do you have a favorite passage of Scripture that calms you when you're distressed?

_____

_____

_____

_____

I wonder why Jesus was so eager to spend this particular Passover with His disciples. The time had come for Him to fulfill the mission for which He'd been born—to die as the sinless Lamb of God, shedding His blood for the forgiveness of our sins. Certainly there were many things He wanted to teach His disciples in those few remaining hours. Yet, His eager desire seemed to be something other than a yearning to teach. Could it be that Jesus needed this time with His friends on that last night?

 Why do you think the fully human part of Jesus might've needed His friends that night?

_____

_____

_____

That night, there were frightening storm clouds hovering on Jesus' horizon: clouds rumbling with coming humiliation; clouds dark with the jeering and cursing that would come when His own people rejected Him and mocked Him; huge clouds filled with the promise of agony and death. Jesus was the Son of God, but He was also the Son of Man. Is it possible, in His humanness, Jesus needed to be surrounded by dear friends who'd give Him love, comfort, and support? Surely He knew the full horror of the dark hours approaching. It's possible He needed the tenderness of sweet fellowship to soothe His aching heart.

Don't stand alone and watch the clouds fill your view. Jesus teaches us to surround ourselves with women who'll uphold us with godly tenderness and love when dark hours approach. Talk to them about the times in the past when God has shown you His love and care. Draw strength from their presence and words of comfort.

Although Jesus might have shuddered at the suffering before Him, He kept His eyes on the prize before Him (Hebrews 12:2). Even though the dark clouds approached, He knew they would pass and He would claim God's promise on the other side of the storm. With these words, Jesus proclaimed that His path through the suffering would culminate in the glory of His kingdom. The earthly Passover ritual to celebrate God's deliverance from slavery would be transformed into a heavenly feast celebrating an eternal deliverance from sin and death for all believers. He would share His joy and His kingdom with His close friends.

As we watch the gathering clouds, what hope can we grasp tightly in our hearts? Certainly we have confidence in an eternity when all suffering will have ended, but we desperately need hope _today_ to carry us through rough days ahead. Our path might lead us into the storm but our feet can stand firm on the many precious promises that soothe our emotions as the storm clouds approach. He promises His enduring presence with us, and that He goes before us (Deuteronomy 31:8). God promises His strength when we face uncertain times (Psalm 28:7), and He's our fortress in difficult times (Psalm 59:16). Even though we stumble through dark days, He's in control of all things, and every event in our lives fulfills His divine purpose

(Ephesians 1:11; Philippians 2:13). We're comforted by these promises because His Word is everlasting and true (Psalms 33:4; Mark 13:31).

What promise of God's work in your life fills you with hope when darkness looms on the horizon?

_____

_____

_____

_____

How our Father fills us with hope in all circumstances! When we draw near to our dear friends, God speaks hope through them. His Word caresses us with the truth of His sovereignty and power (1 Chronicles 29:11–13; Psalm 24:1). When we see the storm approach, we have the peace that, although hail and lightning come from His presence, we can trust our Father in all things.

Dark Clouds Gather

DAY THREE

A GARDEN OF DISTRESS

After sharing this last Passover with His disciples, Jesus withdrew with them to the Garden of Gethsemane, located on the Mount of Olives, near the temple. Luke 22:39 tells us that, when Jesus left the room where they'd celebrated Passover, He *"went out as usual to the Mount of Olives."* Obviously, He often withdrew to this place to pray. As the disciples followed Him, I wonder if they sensed that this time of prayer would be unique. As we follow Jesus into the garden, we can sense the despair that gripped His heart.

> *"They went to a place called Gethsemane, and Jesus said to his disciples, 'Sit here while I pray.' He took Peter, James and John along with him, and he began to be deeply distressed and troubled. 'My soul is overwhelmed with sorrow to the point of death,' he said to them. 'Stay here and keep watch.'"* (Mark 14:32–34)

When they arrived at the garden, I would've expected Jesus to separate Himself from the disciples and go to a secluded area to pray, as was His habit during His ministry (Matthew 14:23). But He didn't do that, did He? He drew aside with His closest friends: Peter, James, and John. In His humanness, Jesus was overcome by His burden and He turned to His closest friends to share it with them.

As they stood there, Jesus opened His heart to them: *"My soul is overwhelmed with sorrow to the point of death."* Jesus wasn't too proud to share His despair and sorrow with them. He wasn't afraid these men would think the Messiah, the very Son of God, was showing weakness. Jesus needed love and comfort from His friends and He reached out for it. By doing that, He shows us it isn't weakness to share our deepest feelings—it's human.

What keeps us from reaching out to our friends? Pride? Embarrassment? Perhaps fear they will ridicule us for a "weak faith"? If Jesus needed to pour out His grief to His friends, how much more do we need to express to our friends the emotions flooding our hearts and minds? The hug of a friend, her tears mingled with ours, and her calm words when we can only rant—these are His gifts to sustain us as the sky darkens.

What emotions fill your heart when dark clouds approach? How does this affect your ability to hear God?

_____

_____

_____

_____

Unfortunately, I'm guilty of letting pride or fear keep me from making a call. Are you? Why do we think we should be able to shoulder things on our own? Do we hesitate to be a burden to someone else—again? When a storm approaches, why do we withdraw into our distress? God blesses us with others who can rejoice with us, weep with us, and pray with us (Romans 12:15).

As Jesus moved away to pray, He asked his friends to remain alert nearby: *"Stay here and keep watch with me"* (Matthew 26:38). Perhaps He was comforted because He knew they were there. Even though He withdrew a distance away from them, He still had the sense He wasn't alone.

"Stay here . . . with me. Just as Jesus needed to feel the presence of His friends, we gain such encouragement when someone is by our side. Perhaps all we need is to feel them nearby and to draw on their strength. Often words aren't even necessary—the important part is that we're not alone.

Have you ever noticed how much more easily you're gripped by panic and despair when you're alone, focusing on the darkness approaching you? We need someone there to lift us up when we stumble over our anxiety (Ecclesiastes 4:10). Satan knows that our weaknesses and fears are magnified when we're without support and protection from those we love and trust. He treads on our hearts until the anguish is out of control. But he can't break through the fortress God builds around us when we're surrounded by the hearts of those we love.

APPLY Sometimes it seems there are no words adequate to calm our souls. When has the simple presence of a friend eased your fear of difficult days ahead?

_____

_____

_____

_____

Several years ago I found myself staring at the results of a mammogram. It said, "ABNORMAL RESULTS. CONTACT YOUR DOCTOR IMMEDIATELY." I can't even describe the terror that my gripped my heart. I assumed the worst and I panicked. Instantly, darkness hovered at the edge of my life. I confided in a close friend who'd walked down that road a few months before. She came and, without words, sat by me with her arm around me. Her presence

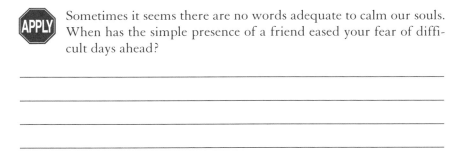

God blesses us with others who can rejoice with us, weep with us, and pray with us.

encouraged me to shift my focus from fear to God, and to grasp on to the truth that He's the God of healing—emotionally and physically. When we're too weakened by panic and fear, Jesus gives us permission, by His actions in Gethsemane, to call our close friends—friends who will draw us back to Him.

PRAYER UNDER A DARKENING SKY

After sharing His deepest emotion with His friends, in great agony, Jesus withdrew to pray.

> *"Going a little farther, he fell to the ground and prayed that if possible the hour might pass from him. 'Abba, Father,' he said, 'everything is possible for you. Take this cup from me. Yet not what I will, but what you will.'"*
> (Mark 14:35, 36)

In these words, does He show us His godliness by meeting with the Father in courage and joy at the task set before Him? No. What a beautiful glimpse this prayer gives us of the humanness of our Savior. What tender intimacy we see between the Son and His Father.

What Jesus said is important, but so is what He did *not* say. Jesus was so burdened with agony He could barely walk, and yet there are no bitter words in His prayer. I've never borne a grief so heavy I couldn't physically stand. But, then, I've never anticipated carrying all mankind's sins on my shoulders.

Look at Jesus' brief words. What did He *not* say that you feel He would have been justified in saying?

_____

_____

_____

_____

What a bitter cup awaited Jesus! He could've cried out, describing the agony He felt. Surely God would've understood, even shed tears with His Beloved. Earlier, Jesus said they were One (John 17:22). Didn't the Father feel the intense pain His Son felt? Jesus, as a human, could've complained, begged that the plan be changed—even scrapped all together. God would've understood. I can't imagine God wanted this any more than Jesus did. God would've reminded Jesus of the plans laid before the creation of the universe—of the desperation of man, forever lost without the shed blood of the perfect Sacrifice only Jesus could be (2 Timothy 1:9, 10). Jesus could've whined and asked, "Why ME?!" Fully human, Jesus could've said all this and more. I certainly would have!

There are four important elements of Jesus' brief prayer. Each reveals the power that prayer can have as we struggle with storms on the horizon. In this prayer, Jesus reveals His full humanity and His full divinity. We've seen the full humanity of Jesus exposed so completely that He turns to His human friends for what only they could give Him: love, support, and companionship. Now we see the fullness of His lordship surrendered to His Father, even to the point of death. He needed His Father's love, strength, and power to be able to face the storms on His horizon.

As women, how often do we stand in our pride and refuse to admit our needs? The world says, "I am woman, Hear me roar!" Even now, Jesus waits for us to surrender to Him. When the storm clouds gather, we must put aside the world's lies and admit we need each other and that we need our loving Jesus. His heart desires to offer us so much: to draw us into His arms and surround us with His love, strength, and peace. He sustains us as we face storms looming in the distance.

Let us look at each element of Jesus' prayer and define the role it played in the restoration of His strength to face the day ahead. As we examine these twenty-one words, phrase by phrase, Jesus Himself will teach us to how to pray when the weight of the world is on our shoulders.

"Abba, Father" . . . Let's dwell on these words for a moment. They reveal much about Jesus' relationship with His Father—and the promise of our relationship with the heavenly Father. *Abba*, an Aramaic word, is an intimate, affectionate term used by children for their fathers. We might use the term "Daddy" or "Papa." As we grow older we might call our earthly father "Dad." These names, just like *Abba*, reflect an intimate love between a father and his child. Jesus did not use this name lightly. In this moment of intense pain, He needed Daddy! He needed to crawl into Daddy's lap and feel safe and loved in a way only His *Abba* could provide for Him.

Can this intimate love be there for us? Can we rightfully pray to the Creator of the universe and call Him *Abba*? Yes, we can! When we come to the cross and allow Jesus to become our Savior, we become God's child, and He becomes our Father (Galatians 3:26). We have a heavenly Daddy to whom we can come with all our joys and tears. He loves us with a depth beyond our understanding, and He yearns to hear us call Him *Abba*. He desires to comfort us and to love us, as any Father desires to comfort His child. Let the words below bathe your heart and mind. Know He's always there for you, just as He was there for His precious Son that night in Gethsemane. He's only a whisper away.

> *"But you received the Spirit of sonship—daughtership, And by him we cry, 'Abba, Father.'"* (Romans 8:15, author's paraphrase)

 For some of us our earthly father was wonderful; for others, memories are painful. What does it mean to you to be able to call the Lord of the universe *Abba*?

_____

_____

_____

Know, however, Jesus did not stop with *Abba*; He also called God "Father." Within the deeply intimate relationship He had with His *Abba*, He never lost view of the reverence and awe with which He must approach His Father. We need to be careful of that, too. As our walk with the Lord God matures, He'll become our Father and a Friend like no other. We'll reveal ourselves to Him in a way we reveal ourselves to no earthly friend, and the

Can we rightfully pray to the Creator of the universe and call Him Abba? Yes, we can!

intimacy of our relationship will deepen day by day. In deep pain or other suffering, it will be easy to go to Him as Daddy and forget He's the Holy of Holies, the Glory of Glories, the Power of Powers. There must always be a reverence, a worshipfulness in our intimacy. He's the Lord God, and Jesus, even in His agony, remained in an attitude of honor and reverence toward His Father.

"Everything is possible for you" . . . What a statement of pure faith! In the dark hours to come, Jesus' closest friends would abandon Him; followers of the Jewish faith who should have embraced Him as Messiah would label Him guilty of heresy. He'd endure humiliation and die an agonizing death for a world who couldn't care less. In spite of this burden, Jesus voiced an affirmation of faith in His Father's control and power that exceeds anything written or spoken in all of Scripture. Jesus placed His life in His Father's hands. Did He trust His Father? Jesus left no room for doubt.

When the advancing storm is too much to bear and we withdraw to pray, Jesus teaches us to declare our faith in God's power! Maybe all we can manage to do is croak, "I think I believe, help me believe more!" (Mark 9:24, author's paraphrase). If we can't think of anything to say, we can sing a praise song or the verse of a wonderful old hymn. Whatever we can manage, we keep repeating it, getting louder every time. Remember, Jesus is the Author of our faith. Slowly He'll stir up faith in our hearts. He'll bring us to our feet, standing on the confidence that He's with us and that He will fulfill His purpose for us, no matter what path we must walk. *Everything is possible with Him!*

He can remove the imposing clouds with but a snap of His fingers. Be aware He probably won't. If He has allowed them to come into our view, He has a purpose for them. Everything is possible for Him. He can remove the advancing clouds or He can guide us through the storm.

Write to your Father a statement of faith you can use when the clouds gather.

_____

_____

_____

_____

_____

_____

Declare your faith in God's power!

Dark Clouds Gather

DAY FIVE

A PRAYER OF SURRENDER

As we study the last words of Jesus' prayer, we will see Him surrender to His Father's will. Part of His surrender is being honest with His Father about the desires of His heart.

"Take this cup from me" . . . What? No question mark? As these words tumbled from His lips, Jesus told it like He wanted it—a statement of His honest

desire: "Take it away!" We don't hear a "Please," "Thank You," or "How-do-you-do?"! Even so, I'm certain Jesus continued to speak with an attitude of honor and reverence. He wasn't afraid to tell His Father what He wanted. Jesus desperately wanted there to be another way to secure our salvation, other than the agony of the cross. He begged His Father to be very sure there was no other way: "There's no 10,000-step program a person can follow to become sinless and righteous before God? There's no gigantic fee that can be paid to purchase a person's forgiveness and right-standing? There's no lifestyle so sacrificial that the suffering will be enough to pay for a person's sins and earn righteousness?" Jesus openly and honestly stated His desire to His Father.

As the Lord's children, we have the privilege of expressing our wants to our Father. Many years ago, my family walked through a crippling crisis. In the early days, as the sky darkened, I spent many hours facedown on the carpet, crying out to the Lord and repeating phrases describing His power. Over and over, I determinedly called on Him and His power to come into that circumstance and declare victory. Although He had many opportunities to do so, the days passed and the storm advanced ever closer. At every twist and turn, I told Him of my desire for deliverance. What a blessed privilege to open my heart's desire to my Father! Was each desire granted? No, but my life and the lives of my loved ones were held close in the arms of my loving Lord.

What heartfelt desire would you express to your Father concerning a past time of suffering or a current storm you see on the horizon?

_____

_____

_____

_____

_____

Have test results for you or a loved one indicated a diagnosis of cancer? Are heavy clouds bearing down on your life, brought on by fear that treatments might not be successful? Fall on your face, as Jesus did, and cry out to your Father, "Take this diagnosis away! Use Your healing power in my life!" Whatever storm builds in the distance, clearly express your desire to God. Be careful to maintain your attitude of reverence. Follow the example of your Jesus, who willingly set aside His own desire in order to be obedient to His Father's will—to die in order that you might be saved.

"Yet not what I will, but what You will" . . . With this phrase, Jesus ended His prayer. He ended where we must end—in complete surrender and obedience to His Father. He'd received comfort from Daddy, He'd expressed His unshakable faith in His Father, and He'd clearly stated His desire. Through it all, He willingly surrendered to the path His Lord called Him to walk.

He didn't selfishly proclaim, as I often do, "If Your path agrees with what I want, then I will do Your will." He set aside His own will; it didn't exist any longer. There'd be no argument and no bargaining. Jesus knew that His Father's will was good and perfect, and He accepted it.

> **As the Lord's children, we have the privilege of expressing our wants to our Father.**

The most difficult thing to accept about God is His sovereignty.

How often I've said the words Jesus uttered, but I'm not sure I've ever truly meant them! Deep in my heart I always want God to see it my way. I lay it all out for Him in utmost logic with three-color diagrams; surely He'll agree with me. How my heart rebels when I hear His gentle voice tell me He'll walk through the storm with me. I never want to walk through it—over it, around it, but never through it! A wise friend once told me the most difficult thing to accept about God is His sovereignty. He is the Lord. He is in complete control. If you and I have been purchased with the blood of His Son, then God the Father is sovereign in our lives. No circumstance is ever allowed into our lives without purpose, without His love, grace, and mercy. Have you trusted Him with your eternal life? If so, trust Him now with your present life.

In what present or past circumstance do you need to trust God and accept His sovereignty?

_____

_____

_____

_____

How can we truly grasp the magnitude of Jesus' prayer? With these words Jesus set in motion an event that would literally alter eternity for all mankind. As light is bent by a prism, so is the eternal destiny of every person who has ever lived bent toward Heaven or Hell based on his or her response to Jesus' work on the cross. Jesus rose from this prayer, ready to face the storm clouds that advanced on His life. His will was brought into agreement with His Father's will and He had surrendered to be the pure, innocent Sacrifice for the sins of all mankind.

How many times, seeing storm clouds approach, have I complained to God, "I don't deserve this hardship! Why aren't You protecting me? You promise protection in Your Word but You aren't giving it!" I've complained the suffering was too much to bear. I'm His child—where is the loving care I "deserve"? I've accused Him of abandoning me in my darkest hour. Have you ever had these thoughts?

We focus on what we "deserve," when we should be asking: What did Jesus deserve? It was the Father's will that His Son face persecution, rejection, and humiliation from the very people He came to save. Did Jesus deserve the painful beatings and the contempt? It was the Father's will that the sinless Son pay the death penalty for the sins of all mankind. Did Jesus deserve to die a horrendous death on the cross for our sins when He had never committed even one sin? Did Jesus deserve to be burdened with our sins and then abandoned by His Father at the moment when He needed Him most?

Perhaps we find ourselves experiencing trials and sufferings we don't deserve. We might suffer when we are innocent. We might experience the death of a friendship, a marriage, a career, or a lifelong dream. We'll occasionally endure the consequences of another person's sin. We'll certainly suffer the consequences of our own sin. But, because of Jesus' sacrifice, we will never endure suffering to the extent we deserve. Through it all, we have the right to complain to our Father; we can cry out that the suffering is too much. He will listen; He'll comfort and strengthen us as we go through the experience. We can tell Jesus all about it—He will guide us through the storm because He's been there!

One thing we will never experience: Our Father will never abandon us. He'll remain with us and within us and will surround us every moment of every day, through the person of the Holy Spirit (John 14:15–17). Jesus experienced God's wrath so we never will (Romans 5:9–11). If Jesus is our Savior, our sins are cleansed, removed as far as the east is from the west—God sees them no more, remembers them no more. We are pure and perfect in His eyes and He has promised to never leave us. We will never face a minute without His presence.

APPLY How has this discussion changed your perspective of God's sover-iegnty in difficult times that approach your life?

_____

_____

_____

_____

Surrendering to our Father's will is so easy when He brings fair skies and gentle breezes! We never question Him on beautiful days—sadly, we often forget to thank Him! Beautiful days are taken for granted, as though they are due us. Then, as we gaze out on the glorious horizon, we become aware of a small cloud. It continues to build and others, dark and ominous, cluster around it. We cry out, as though it's unfair. Somewhere, deep in our hearts, God whispers, "I've been in control all along. I desire you to come to Me every day, on beautiful days as well as stormy ones."

We never face a minute without God's presence.

Notes

5

When the Storm Strikes

*I*t's impossible! We were praying. Armies of believers were praying. The storm hit anyway, full force.

An "ever-faithful" husband stomped out of counseling, walked straight into the arms of another woman, and then demanded a divorce.

Your cat got in a stupid cat fight over the weekend; the vet bill's staggering. More on the charge card!

Where do we go for support for our sixteen-year-old pregnant daughter . . . and for us?

The old refrigerator finally bit the dust and the money just isn't there for a new one.

How our faith is shaken when the storm hits! We watch distant clouds rush closer and closer, and we tumble into despair when the darkness begins to settle in around us. We plead for Him to take the storm away, and when it continues to rage, we feel abandoned.

As we turn to God and His Word, we find assurance He's with us. His presence envelops us, even as the driving rain and high winds begin to batter our lives. Let's follow God as He walks into the life of Gideon, a young man who faced dark days and learned of God's presence and power.

A SHAKEN FAITH

A Man after My Own Heart

The early days of a storm are an emotional roller coaster. Shock, anger, and confusion assault the emotions—and, in the meantime, all that's left is the deadness of exhaustion. Satan seizes this opportunity to slink in, armed with the blackness of doubt, knowing we're too weak and confused to resist him. His goal is to cause us to question God's love and presence. This struggle is where we find one of my favorite men in Scripture, Gideon, whose story is told in Judges 6–8. I love Gideon because he reacts to the storm ravaging his little household the same way I would. As we study this passage, be prepared to laugh a little at Gideon, and perhaps at yourself. Be ready to be amazed at the loving way our Lord responds to Gideon.

When Gideon was a young man, Israel was deep in a cycle of disobedience to the Lord (Judges 2:16–23). They worshiped the false gods of the region, Baal and Asherah, and the Israelite men just couldn't resist the pretty pagan women living around them. To get Israel's attention, God allowed a nearby nation, Midian, to invade Israel and oppress the people (Judges 6:1). Now, ladies, God didn't snap his fingers and create Midian's invading army out of thin air just to torment Israel. Nations invading nations was the sport of the times, and Midian was the regional champion. God chose to use Midian to discipline His people.

When Midian invaded Israel, Gideon lived in his father's household (Judges 6:11, 30). Along with the rest of Israel, Joash led his family to worship Baal and Asherah (Judges 6:25). Worshipping other gods is idolatry: It wasn't acceptable to the Lord then, it wasn't acceptable to Jesus (Matthew 6:24), and it isn't acceptable now. Along with the rest of Israel, Joash's household suffered under the oppression of the Midianites. This is where the story of Gideon begins.

Eventually, Gideon would become a mighty judge for the nation of Israel (Judges 8:28), but his journey didn't have such an auspicious beginning. At this point, he was a frightened, miserable young man. Have you ever sat mindlessly, afraid to face the day? Well, that's how Gideon felt as he hid in the winepress. He was frightened of the Midianites and had run out of hope. Into this circumstance stepped the Lord.

> *"The angel of the LORD came and sat down under the oak in Ophrah that belonged to Joash the Abiezrite, where his son Gideon was threshing wheat in a winepress to keep it from the Midianites."* (Judges 6:11)

I'm a city girl, but I do know the difference between wine and wheat. I can't imagine what you would do with wheat in a winepress. Yet, there Gideon was, threshing wheat in a winepress. A look at the ancient processes of threshing wheat and making wine shows us how futile Gideon's actions were.

After harvesting, workers took wheat to the threshing floor, a large, flat space generally on top of a hill. They threw the sheaves of wheat in a big pile on the threshing floor to be trod on by teams of donkeys or oxen dragging large stones. Workers then tossed the grain up in the air to allow the wind to blow away the lighter chaff (husks) and straw, while the heavier grain fell to the threshing floor. All this activity was hard to hide—and it was very dangerous. The Midianites were known for stealing the grain after all the work had been done to thresh it.

In contrast, the winepresses were near the vineyards down in the valley. A winepress was a large vat, two or three feet deep, either cut into solid rock or dug into the earth and then tightly lined with stones. Baskets of grapes picked from the vines were emptied into the winepress and workers stomped on them to release the juice. (This is the part that's always done with such gusto in the movies!) The juice was then allowed to ferment, becoming wine.

Now, it's pretty easy to see how threshing wheat down in a vat wouldn't work very well. Gideon would have to beat on the sheaves with a rock to loosen the grain. And there couldn't be much wind down in a hole in the ground, to blow away the chaff. This isn't a very logical place to find our hero, Gideon. But the winepress was a place where he could huddle and do the best he could as he endured the storm.

How Gideon's heart must have pounded as he hid in the winepress and strained to hear the sounds of the Midianite raiding parties! Did he pray? I'm sure he did, but to whom? He'd grown up worshipping many gods: Baal, Asherah, and the God of Israel. Did he pray to Baal and Asherah, asking for courage and deliverance? Perhaps he prayed to God and accused Him of abandoning his people when they needed Him most. God heard Gideon's prayers. He even heard the prayers lifted to those false gods. God came to Gideon, even though he was mixing idolatry with the worship of the true God.

Gideon's emotions must have been like a whirlwind. He was probably frightened, frustrated, and without hope. Wouldn't this be a great time for self-pity? Can you imagine how Gideon might've whined as he huddled in that winepress? He probably whined about the Midianites. He might've whined about how unfair life was. Perhaps he whined because no one was helping him with his wheat. Gideon was so focused on his fear and self-pity, he didn't notice the angel of the Lord who sat under the oak tree and watched him. Gideon had given up, and he was completely unaware of God's presence in the form of the angel.

Can you identify with Gideon? I certainly can. We, too, tend to turn to the false gods in our lives before we turn to God. We all have them: stubbornness, self-sufficiency, and the desire to be in control. We turn to friends for comfort and encouragement instead of turning to God. Yes, God can use our Christian friends to strengthen our faith in a time of need, but they should never become a substitute for God.

When have you turned to friends or "false gods" to ease your fear and build your strength?

_____

_____

_____

We only see God's work in our lives when we take our eyes off our circumstances and look at Him.

Many years ago, a storm struck my life. God had given me a dear Christian friend who encouraged me and prayed for me. One particularly difficult day, I longed for the calming sound of my friend's voice and automatically reached out to pick up the phone. As I picked up the receiver, I heard God's Spirit whisper to my heart: "You run to hear her voice but you haven't turned to Me for comfort and strength." I put down the receiver and prayed to the Lord of comfort. Was it wrong to turn to my friend? No, in fact God had given her to me for that very reason. But He never intended for her to become a substitute for prayer and fellowship with Him.

Have you ever noticed that self-pity often leads to whining? We can whine for hours. "It's not fair, I don't deserve this." "Nobody else is in this mess. Why is God picking on me?" "I don't want to do this, it's too hard." How self-destructive self-pity can be! We wallow in our sorrow and we lose sight of God. If He were to walk right up to us, would we be so busy whining that we didn't even notice Him? We only see God's work in our lives when we take our eyes off our circumstances and look at Him.

 How does God minister to you when you're submerged in self-pity?

_____

_____

_____

God is patient to teach us as the storm enters our lives. It is futile to turn to any other god. No other god is sovereign. No other god is able to meet our every need. Our Father calms the roller coaster of emotion and fills us with peace. He delivers us from the trap of self-pity and gives us the strength to focus on Him. When we lift our eyes and become aware of His presence, we are filled with hope.

Dark Clouds Gather

DAY TWO

MIGHTY WARRIOR?

"When the angel of the LORD appeared to Gideon, he said, "The LORD is with you, mighty warrior." (Judges 6:12)

The Lord didn't wait for Gideon to notice His angel. Can you imagine how stunned and panicked Gideon was when an angel appeared at the edge of the winepress and spoke to him? Don't miss the power of the words the angel spoke.

"The LORD Is with You"
God knew Gideon's thoughts, just as he knows yours. He heard the questions: Where is God? Why has God abandoned me? He knew just what Gideon needed to hear: *"The LORD is with you."*

When have you felt abandoned by God? Do you perhaps feel abandoned now?

_____

_____

_____

_____

Dear one, you are *never* abandoned by God. He's always with you, within you, surrounding you. Complete the verses below and allow the truth of God's Word to assure you of His presence.

"And surely I am with you _____, to the _____ _____ of the age." (Matthew 28:20)

"_____ will I _____ you; _____ will I _____ you." (Hebrews 13:5)

As the mountains _____ Jerusalem, so the LORD *_____ his people both now and _____.* (Psalm 125:2)

God is with you. He'll never leave you. His love and care will surround you forever. Yet it's easy to forget that fact when the storm rages around you. Sometimes it's easier to believe He is not there than to accept that He has allowed this suffering.

When a dark storm of suffering invaded my family, I questioned whether God was present. My prayers seemed to go unanswered day after day. God seemed to allow the very worst outcome in every situation. I felt I was being abandoned by my heavenly Father. I read aloud Scripture passages promising His continuous presence with me and accused Him of breaking these promises. How dare He abandon me! How could I possibly face the storm without Him? My fear, anger, and hopelessness were raw and painful; I took it all out on Him. In the midst of all this pain, God knew just what I needed to hear: *"The Lord is with you."*

Gideon didn't have Scripture to turn to as he struggled with a sense of abandonment but he did have the stories of God's miraculous deliverance. As he worked futilely in the winepress, did he complain to God because His past deliverance wasn't much help now? Did he accuse God of turning His back on his people? Did Gideon think he wasn't good enough for God's love and care? Into this feeling of abandonment and fear, the Lord sent an angel to confirm to Gideon that God's eyes were upon him. In the midst of the storm, God's eyes are upon you and His hand is over you, even as the psalmist proclaims:

"Even the sparrow has found a home, and the swallow a nest for herself, where she may have her young—a place near your altar, O LORD *Almighty, my King and my God."* (Psalm 84:3)

The View through God's Eyes
Gideon was very critical of himself. Can you imagine him thinking, "How can I be so weak? A *real* man wouldn't be cowering down here in a pit. I'm a spineless coward." Did God hear Gideon's thoughts? Of course! He sent an angel to lift Gideon's spirit and encourage Gideon to see himself through God's eyes. Only God could encourage Gideon and give him strength. Once the angel had affirmed the presence of the Lord, he looked at Gideon and addressed him as "mighty warrior." Every time I read this passage, I laugh. Mighty warrior? Here was Gideon, the mighty warrior, hiding in a hole in

the ground and hoping for a little wind as he tossed handfuls of grain in the air. Gideon looked at his weakness. The angel looked at him—the Lord looked at Gideon—and saw him as he could be—and would be—not as he was at that moment.

What was Gideon's view of himself (Judges 6:15)? How does that compare with the Lord's view of him as a "mighty warrior"?

_____

_____

_____

Gideon didn't see himself as a mighty warrior. The Hebrew phrase used in Judges 6:12 means a "warrior or champion who keeps the people safe."[9] Gideon didn't see himself as a strong, brave warrior; he was hiding in a winepress. He didn't see himself as one who would keep his people safe from the Midianites; he was scared to death of them. He allowed himself to be overcome by his circumstances. He listened to the whispers and murmurs of Satan, telling him he was too weak and frightened to stand up to the Midianites. Gideon was defeated and without hope. He hid in the winepress in despair. Praise God, our Father didn't leave him there!

As you think about past or present crises, what lies has the Enemy told you, making you doubt yourself?

_____

_____

_____

Just as the Lord came to Gideon to reveal Gideon's true identity in the Lord's eyes, He comes to us in His Word to give us the same truths. He will not leave us, lost in lies the Enemy has told us. Why are we so eager to believe the negative about ourselves? When I was a child, my father told me I was stupid, worthless, and hopeless. He told me I'd never amount to anything. In contrast, my mother told me I was smart and wonderful. I chose to believe the negative and it almost destroyed my life. My view of myself did not match the truth of God's Word.

Before I came to Jesus, I was dead in my sins, like a bundle of filthy rags (Isaiah 64:6; Colossians 2:13). But I wasn't worthless! It wasn't true I'd never amount to anything. My worth and yours can be measured in Jesus' blood as it dripped from the cross. My heavenly Father considered me—and you—to be of such immense worth He sacrificed His only Son to bring us a new life in Him. My mind still cannot grasp the wonder of it. I'm a child of the King—I, who "would never amount to anything"! I'm my heavenly Father's treasured possession (Deuteronomy 26:18; Titus 2:14) and a new creation in Him (2 Corinthians 5:17). This is who I am and I'll cling to this identity for eternity. If you've not embraced God and allowed Him to re-create you, please do so now.

 How does the Lord's view of you compare with your view of yourself?

_____

_____
_____
_____

Lift your eyes and remember: You are a child of the King!

The Lord didn't leave me with those lies, and He won't leave you with the lies this world may tell you! Satan is the father of lies (John 8:44) and our Father is Truth (Psalm 31:5). When God looks at you, He sees your true identity. Does Satan tell you you're defeated by past sins and weaknesses? Father God calls you by your true identity in Jesus: a _Holy Person, the Redeemed of the Lord_ (Isaiah 62:12). Does Satan tell you the Lord no longer wants you because of past failures? Father God calls you the one who is _"Sought after"_ (Isaiah 62:12), Does Satan tell you God doesn't care about you? Father God calls you His child and an heir to His inheritance (Romans 8:16, 17)! The onset of a storm doesn't change who you are in Christ! The onset of a storm may cause you to pull your eyes off Jesus and onto your circumstances, but it hasn't changed who you are. Lift your eyes and remember: You are a child of the King!

BELIEF OR DESPAIR?

When the Storm Strikes

DAY THREE

"But sir," Gideon replied, "if the LORD is with us, why has all this happened to us? Where are all his wonders that our fathers told us about when they said, 'Did not the LORD bring us up out of Egypt?' But now the LORD has abandoned us and put us into the hand of Midian." (Judges 6:13)

If . . . one small word that held all of Gideon's doubts. _If_ the Lord were there, He'd never allow the Midianites to invade Israel and to oppress them. _If_ the Lord were there, He'd never desert Gideon in the bottom of a winepress. When Gideon couldn't see the reason for the suffering, he doubted God's presence.

"Why has this happened?" Gideon saw the destruction around him and blamed God. The oppression said to him that God's promises of protection were empty words. He didn't realize Israel's disobedience was the cause of their misery. It wasn't God's actions that put the Israelites into the hands of the Midianites—it was Israel's idolatry.

"Why?" This is the question that drove our parents insane when we were toddlers. "Why?" has spilled from our lips as long as we can remember and we take this question to God when things fall apart. How many times have you asked, "Why's God allowing this to happen to me?" When we can't pay the bills, when a loved one is seriously ill, or when our teens are out of control, we cry out, "Why, Lord?"

When have you cried out to God, asking "Why?" how did He minister to you?

_____
_____
_____
_____

In my own life, I remember a dark time when my family fought the terrible destruction of an outsider's lies. One evening I sat, sobbing uncontrollably and whispering repeatedly, "Why, Lord?" Then I heard His Spirit speak to my desperate heart: "What if I were to tell you one million people will come to know Jesus Christ as their Savior because of this tragedy—would that give you peace, and quiet your questions?"

I wish I could say my desire to see the lost come to know Jesus was greater than my selfishness, but it's not true. I said, out loud, "No! It's not good enough!" My Father, in His loving kindness, understood my deep feelings. He understood why my desire for the deliverance of my family overruled everything else. Lovingly He took me to Scripture to teach me that He could not explain "why" to me. His thoughts and plans were beyond my understanding.

> *"For my thoughts are not your thoughts, neither are your ways my ways," declares the LORD. "As the heavens are higher than the earth, so are my ways higher than your ways and my thoughts than your thoughts."* (Isaiah 55:8, 9)

I couldn't understand why it was necessary for my family to walk through that dark valley. His purposes were beyond my comprehension. But I could sit there and pour out my raw emotions. I received not only His tender love and comfort, but also a greater capacity to trust Him.

After the time of suffering ended, my family tried to put our lives back together and to allow the Lord to heal our broken hearts. Sometime later, one of my daughters went on an international mission trip. When she returned, she shared with me her experiences and described how her testimony about our family's difficulty had resulted in the salvation of a young man about her age. We both remembered that desperate evening when I'd sobbed before the Lord. She looked at me and said, "Mom, he's the first in our one million!" Did I continue to ask, "Why?" Sure, but I'm thankful to the Lord for allowing us to see the firstfruits of our suffering.

We tend to measure God's love and presence by watching what He does.

Have you doubted God's presence because He didn't do what you wanted Him to do? We tend to measure God's love and presence by watching what He does. God never says, "Seek my hands." We are told to , *"Seek His face always"* (2 Chronicles 7:14; also see Psalm 27:8). When we take our eyes off our circumstances and seek God's face, He'll turn toward us and fill us with assurance. Read the verses below and bathe in the joy His face brings into our lives, even during the struggle.

> *"The LORD make his* face *shine upon you and be gracious to you; the LORD turn his* face *toward you and give you peace."* (Numbers 6:25, 26)

> *"Look to the LORD and his strength; seek his* face *always."* (1 Chronicles 16:11)

> *"Let your* face *shine on your servant; save me in your unfailing love."* (Psalm 31:16)

> *"Restore us, O God; make your* face *shine upon us, that we may be saved."* (Psalm 80:3)

> *"I have sought your* face *with all my heart; be gracious to me according to your promise."* (Psalm 119:58)

APPLY How has God's face shone upon you as you struggled through hardship?

_____

_____

_____

_____

How beautiful is our Lord's face! He smiles upon us in grace and gives us peace. He fills us with His strength and with His unfailing love. When we seek His face we're assured all His promises are true. Why do we turn to the face of those with knowledge and try to learn our way out of the storm? Why do we turn to the world for advice on how to face our circumstances bravely? Nothing can lift our hearts and give us courage as can the face of our Father.

To Gideon, it seemed natural to question God's presence. All through his childhood, he'd heard about the miracles the Lord performed when He delivered the children of Israel from bondage in Egypt. His faith in God was based on the stories of those past miracles. He expected miracles. Maybe he believed God owed them miracles. When they didn't come, His faith crashed.

Aren't we all like Gideon? We look back into our past and see times when God reached down from His throne and yanked us right out of danger. He did it then, so He's supposed to do it now. Although the memory of God's work in past circumstances should increase our faith in Him, we can't demand He meet our expectations. Yes, He is the same yesterday, today, and tomorrow (Hebrews 13:8). No, His work in each circumstance isn't the same. His purpose in one situation might be to show us His power; His purpose for another might be to teach us His faithfulness.

As you consider a past or present trial, what might God be teaching you?

_____

_____

_____

_____

Don't make the same mistake Gideon did. He remembered the miracles and wonders from the past and, because he saw no miracles in the present, he assumed God had abandoned him. God was a God of miracles; He's still a God of miracles! Should we judge His presence based on the presence or absence of miraculous deliverance? No! We must ask God to show us His presence, even as the storm rolls into our lives. Just as He did with the children of Israel, God has a purpose for every storm entering our lives. He shows us His presence and gives us His guidance. He speaks to us through a word said by a friend, a song heard on the radio, or a seemingly insignificant event. As you go through the early days of a storm, keep your heart open to the still, small, gentle voice of God.

> _Nothing can lift our hearts and give us courage as can the face of our Father._

> _As you go through the early days of a storm, keep your heart open to the still, small, gentle voice of God._

PARALYZED BY DOUBT

"The LORD turned to him and said, 'Go in the strength you have and save Israel out of Midian's hand. Am I not sending you?' 'But Lord,' Gideon asked, 'how can I save Israel? My clan is the weakest in Manasseh, and I am the least in my family.' The LORD answered, 'I will be with you, and you will strike down all the Midianites together.'" (Judges 6:14-16)

Although we might not realize it, the conversation between God and Gideon in Judges 6:14–16 happens many times in our lives. The storm arrives, God says, "Go through it," and we blubber with excuses. We stammer, "Send this crisis to someone stronger; maybe that prayer warrior I admire so much. She has the faith to handle it!"

To be fair, God hadn't given Gideon a clue about the real reason for His visit. They'd discussed whether Gideon was a man or a mouse and debated the question of God's presence. Gideon then accused God of abandonment. Now God drops a bombshell on poor Gideon.

"Go in the strength you have and save Israel out of Midian's hand." Seemingly, out of nowhere, God told Gideon to climb up out of the winepress, put his fighting clothes on, and go defeat the Midianites. God's words must've stunned Gideon. It's interesting how God phrased that—*"go in the strength you* have."

This seems a little contradictory to the spiritual truths we have: God and God alone is the source of our strength and we can do nothing without Him (Psalm 28:6–9; John 15:5). Obviously God saw something in Gideon that Gideon himself didn't see. What qualities did Gideon demonstrate that might've helped him as he walked from one storm to another?

Certainly Gideon was determined and resourceful. He refused to allow his family to go hungry. Who would think of threshing wheat in a winepress? He cared deeply for his family and for his nation. And just think about his conversation with God. He may have been afraid of the Midianites but he wasn't too afraid of an angel to challenge his words! Perhaps Gideon was braver than he thought. He had many God-given qualities that gave him strength, even though they were buried under his weaknesses.

What God-given qualities do you have that give you strength and courage to face the battle?

_____

_____

_____

_____

It's hard to acknowledge our own good qualities. We tend to focus on the negative. When the storm comes, we cry out that we can't bear it. Yet we have many God-given qualities He can use to bring us through the turmoil. We are so buried under our weaknesses we never see ourselves through God's eyes. When I look at myself, I see impatience, stubbornness, and a tendency to organize the fire out of everything (I even alphabetize my spices). And then there's this little matter of wanting to be in control all the time.

What weaknesses do you see in yourself that God can turn into strengths?

_____

_____

_____

_____

Only God has the power to create strength out of my weaknesses. He transforms my impatience into persistence: I won't stop praying until I see His work in my situation. He molds my stubbornness into determination: I am dead set on making it through! And nobody can organize a Scripture list that applies to my circumstances like I can. I write them out on index cards and carry them with me to read when panic sets in. And my desire to be in control? He teaches me to be a fighter—to hold on to Him and not let go until we come out the other side. Through His grace, I emerge from the turmoil a new creation.

Notice Gideon didn't leap out of the winepress and utter a war cry. He sat there, paralyzed by fear and doubt. He doubted himself: He couldn't do it. He doubted God's plan—was He going to send Gideon out on his own? Instead he stammered, *"But Lord . . ."* If I had a penny for every time I said that, I could retire.

Gideon knew how ferocious the storm lying before him could be. The best he could hope for was a rag-tag group of men going to battle against a well-organized Midianite army. So he decided it was time to convince God he couldn't handle it. Gideon explained to God that his family was poor and insignificant. They couldn't possibly convince Israel to rise up and defeat Midian. And besides, Gideon was the weakest of the weak and the smallest of the small. Essentially, he said to God: "You can't chose anyone worse than me!" He immediately informed God he didn't have what it took to survive.

How have you tried to convince God you can't handle the storm you're facing?

_____

_____

_____

When the storm hits my life, I want to join Gideon in the winepress. I'm sure God expects too much of me—I can't make it through. I spout all kinds of reasons why I can't endure such a calamity: I'm already pressured at work and I can't handle anything else; I'm tithing so I can't afford the car repair bill; my elderly Mom depends on me and I can't deal with my own illness. He just can't expect me to deal with any more.

So, I ask Him to quiet the wind and calm the seas. I boldly expect a miracle. I tell Him to fix it! But where's the faith that He will get me through it? Where's the trust that He is in control? If I'll be quiet for a minute, I'll hear Him say the same thing to me He said to Gideon: *"I will be with you."*

> **Only God has the power to create strength out of our weaknesses.**

No matter what the future brings, you have this promise: "I will be with you."

Dear one, you are never without His presence. You can never escape His faithfulness. As you wade though financial problems, He whispers, *"I will be with you."* When you dread the night hours that overwhelm you with loneliness, He assures you, *"I will be with you."* No matter what the future brings, you have this promise: *"I will be with you."*

Even as God promises His presence, the question becomes, Will we be with Him? Will we choose to be accompanied by fear and doubt rather than His peace? Will we choose to listen to Satan's voice rather than God's? Jesus will never deny you free choice. When a storm strikes and emotions begin to build, He'll allow you to choose the voice that attracts your ear. He'll allow you to choose your companions. His heart's desire is for you turn to Him, giving your deepest emotions to Him. He'll share the burden with you and bring healing to your heart. The downward spiral never has to begin. Trust Him with your heart.

How we long for victory! We want to see illnesses healed and marriages restored. We want to see the storm clouds part and those who attack us defeated. We want what Gideon got: the promise of a victory over the Midianites—a visible victory. Let the world around us marvel as we overcome our hardships in the same way the Midianites were amazed at Israel's stunning triumph.

God promises us victory as well, but it's not always a victory the world will recognize. When our faith strengthens as the storm builds, that's a victory. When others see our peace and joy in spite of the storm, that's a victory. Those might not be the kind of victories we want but they're victories that are eternal.

 When have you experienced God's victory, one that the eyes of the world never recognize?

_____

_____

_____

_____

When the Storm Strikes

DAY FIVE

FROM DESPAIR TO VICTORY

Even though he heard God's words and His promises, Gideon doubted that the Lord could use him. He was still buried in his emotions. Fear . . . self-criticism . . . feelings of abandonment. How could he possibly save Israel—he was the least of the least, the weakest of the weakest. Gideon was caught in a downward spiral and his faith was paralyzed.

How many times do your thoughts follow those of Gideon as he hid in the winepress? The storm hits, and at first, you're shocked and hurt. How can God possibly allow you to suffer? Then comes the doubt. Is He with you as He promised? Is He aware of what's happening? Doubt soon gels into cold, hard fear. You can't make it through this! God expects you to be strong but you can't . . .

Many days I've lost control of my emotions. Like me, have you felt yourself falling into a dark pit of despair? Who can rescue you? Who can lift your soul? Jesus can! Listen to the psalmist:

> *"The cords of death entangled me, the anguish of the grave came upon me; I was overcome by trouble and sorrow."* (Psalm 116:3)

The word the psalmist used for "grave" is the Hebrew word "Sheol," the name of the underworld, where the unrighteous spend eternity separated from God. He used such an extreme word to express the darkness of his despair. Even though he felt misery and desperation, he knew he could trust God to hear his prayer and deliver him.

> *"I love the LORD, for he heard my voice; he heard my cry for mercy."* (Psalm 116:1)

When Gideon found himself ensnared in a pit of hopelessness, he had no faith in God's salvation. Because he saw no evidence of miracles in his own time, he began to believe the lie Satan whispered: "God has abandoned His people!" The hurt of abandonment became doubt—if God has broken His promise to be with His people, are any of His promises true? Doubt soon became fear; "If God's not with us, we're done for!" As Gideon cringed in the winepress, he was entangled in the cords described in Psalm 116:3. He had descended from hurt to doubt to fear, but unlike the psalmist, he had no hope of God's deliverance.

When hurt comes, give your tears to Jesus—before doubt can form. Jesus understands hurt; He understands feeling betrayed. A man He loved for three years betrayed Him with a kiss (Luke 22:47, 48). Pour your hurt out to Him. His comfort will bring victory over your pain.

Are you struggling with the overwhelming emotion of a present difficulty or the pain of a past trial? Express it here; give it to Jesus and allow His comfort to bring you victory.

_____

_____

_____

_____

_____

_____

_____

God's love surrounded us before we knew Him and it will endure forever (Psalm 100:5; Romans 5:8). His love doesn't guarantee us a life free of suffering; in fact, Jesus promised that His followers would endure hardship upon hardship (Luke 6:22; John 16:33). At the risk of sounding harsh, demanding an easy life as proof of God's love only reveals our selfishness. "Prosperity Christianity" teaches that Jesus will give us a life of roses and riches. It's been a popular belief for centuries—and it's been a false teaching for centuries. Listen to the apostle Paul describe life in Jesus:

> *"I have been crucified with Christ and I no longer live, but Christ lives in me. The life I live in the body, I live by faith in the Son of God, who loved me and gave himself for me."* (Galatians 2:20)

> **In times of suffering, God's goals are to refine you, to see you become all you can be, and then to reveal Himself to others through your life.**

When suffering comes and the pain you feel causes you to doubt God, remember these words: You " have been crucified with Christ." Your will, your goals, your dreams, and your desire for pleasure—all these have been crucified. Jesus now lives His life within you and through you. In times of suffering, God's goals are to refine you, to see you become all you can be, and then to reveal Himself to others through your life. His very presence in your life proves He loves you. His desire to perfect you proves He cares for you. He gave Himself for you in extreme suffering. Every moment you spend in suffering is a moment you share with Him, in an intimacy you can gain no other way (Philippians 3:10). It doesn't make it fun; but the pain is tempered by a joy found in the deepening love relationship between you and your Savior.

When the way's hard, doubt comes to all of us. Don't hesitate to take your questions to Him and He'll reveal Himself to you and give you peace. Do it immediately, before doubt can harden into fear. Doubts aren't sin when they're only questions; they become sin when you refuse to look to God for answers. Ask Jesus to answer your doubts. Only Jesus can calm your doubts and bring you peace.

APPLY What doubts have caused turmoil in your mind during a past or present crisis? How has Jesus calmed your heart and brought you peace?

_____

_____

_____

_____

Remember—Satan's the author of confusion. In the midst of heartache, he loves to whisper things to us to make us doubt what we know to be truth. When we doubt God's love, His presence, and His promises, Satan gains a victory. When we try to pray, doubts swirl through our thoughts and block our prayers. When we try to read Scripture, doubts creep into our minds and blur the words. Peace seems impossible, yet His Word promises us peace:

> *"And the peace of God, which transcends all understanding, will guard your hearts and minds in Christ Jesus."* (Philippians 4:7)

What an amazing promise this verse brings! It promises God's peace, His perfect peace (Isaiah 26:3). Man's peace, the world's peace, can be shattered by one careless word, but God's peace rests on His power and faithfulness. When He speaks peace into your heart and mind, Satan's confusion melts away and a peace that defies all logic floods your soul. Jesus, the Prince of Peace, will rule in your heart and mind, and all those around you will be amazed at the calm in you as you weather the storm. You won't understand it. Those around you won't understand it. And God will be given the glory.

The most beautiful part of God's promise in Philippians 4:7 is found in the word "guard." This Greek word means a sentinel who is "to keep or to protect, preserve spiritually."[10] Once God's peace is established, it becomes a sentinel that continuously guards your heart and mind, and it's sustained by the power and presence of the Holy Spirit. God's peace guards you against Satan's attack of lies and confusion. It guards you against worldly influences. It guards you against your own weakness that might allow your circumstances to become overwhelming. God's peace acts as a shield to guard you against the arrows of doubt the Enemy fires at you. Express your doubts, trading them for unbelievable peace.

Left alone, doubts will lead to fear; but, even then, all is not lost. When you're paralyzed in fear, Jesus will free you if you call on Him. Jesus conquered death; He can conquer your fear. God said, *"So do not fear, for I am with you"* (Isaiah 41:10a). I know these words are easier to read than to believe when difficulties surround you. Satan's counting on this. It's his desire for you to stay conquered by fear. You are standing between Satan's temptation to stay in fear and Jesus' call to freedom. Which will you choose?

What fears have held you in bondage during difficult times? How have you been able to respond to Jesus' call to freedom?

_____

_____

_____

_____

_____

Bondage or freedom—it would seem to be an open-and-shut case, wouldn't it? But the need to take a step from the shadows of fear causes a whole new level of apprehension. Fear's not a place you want to be, but it's a place you know, and that makes it a place that's somewhat comfortable. Satan knows how to make fear seem cozy. He can make the bars and chains that imprison you fade into the background. He'll make you forget he's already been defeated by Jesus' death and resurrection (John 16:11; Hebrews 2:14, 15). Because God has chosen not to eternally condemn him until the final day of judgment, Satan's still here to harass us. But our hope is found in this magnificent truth: *"The one who is in you is greater than the one who is in the world"* (1 John 4:4).

Jesus Himself is within in you, through the indwelling of the Holy Spirit. Romans 8:15 promises that you haven't been given a spirit that makes you a slave of fear. The Spirit embodies all Jesus' power, glory, wisdom, love, and tenderness. His power is infinitely greater than Satan's power. His wisdom overcomes Satan's lies. His love and tenderness melt any fear caused by Satan. All this is available to you, even if you're so overwhelmed you can't feel it. Jesus knows how hard it is to walk out of fear's darkness on your own. Turn to trusted friends He has placed around you. Allow them to pray with you, releasing His power into your life. There've been many times when Jesus' healing power poured into my heart through the prayers of a faithful friend.

How easy it is to withdraw and to choose darkness; many times, I've done just that! Even when you're dwelling in the depths of blackness, Jesus is there. He won't allow you to remain there forever, if you belong to Him. He has been and still is victorious over every dark place, every despairing moment. All of us have been enslaved with the chains of fear, pain, despair, or other of Satan's lies. But there will come a time when God will declare, "Enough!" His strong arms will reach into the darkness of your captivity and He'll lift you tenderly to carry you into the light. You'll feel your

Jesus has been and still is victorious over every dark place, every despairing moment.

strength return and your hope be renewed. Praise God, you're never in a place so black and so deep His mighty arms cannot reach you (Deuteronomy 26:8)! Jesus lifts those crippled by despair every day:

> *"'Woman, you are set free from your infirmity.' Then he put his hands on her, and immediately she straightened up and praised God"* (Luke 13:12, 13).

6

One Step at a Time

We live by faith, not by sight. (2 Corinthians 5:7) Live? Who's living? At the peak of a storm, life is lost in the struggle just to stand and face each new day. Faith? Who has any left? Unanswered prayers have drained my faith. Sight? Who can see in this storm? Eyes strain, searching for a glimmer of hope. That's my reaction to those words when the storm is raging and I'm holding on for dear life. Have you ever felt that way?

But, wait . . . peer through the pouring rain. Can you see Him? It's Jesus, walking toward you on the floodwaters surrounding your life. He's bringing you strength to live in this moment, a new song of faith to sing, and plastic goggles in your favorite color to keep the rain out of your eyes! He's coming to lead you through the worst of the storm, one step at a time.

As we go through chapters 6 and 7, you'll have several opportunities to use a Faith Focus card to record Scripture verses that will strenghten and encourage you as you stumble through today's storms and those that might come in the furure. The Faith Focus Card is provided for you as a perforated card at the back of your book. Your group leader will also have cards to give you during your session on Chapter 5.

(Additional cards are available at sherrycarter.com/books.html) Do you have your walking shoes on? Faith is only a step away.

STORMY STEPS AHEAD

There was a time when I'd emptied myself out to God: every emotion, every thought, until I was numb. But the storm kept raging. I was just a shell, going through the motions. I moved blindly through my responsibilities, I was unfeeling in relationships, and I seemed to pray in vain. Only one thing kept me moving from day to day: the words of Deuteronomy 31:8:

"The LORD himself goes before you and will be with you; he will never leave you nor forsake you. Do not be afraid; do not be discouraged."

I kept telling myself, "The Lord is going before me in this horrible mess. He's with my family every step of the way. He won't leave us. I don't have to be afraid." But I *was* terrified, and I felt abandoned. I tried pep talks: "I don't have to be discouraged when everything seems to go wrong." "God knows the final outcome and He's already victorious." But I *was* discouraged. I felt hopeless and defeated. I tried to take my eyes off my circumstances and to focus them on the truth of His Word. I tried to surrender my heart and mind to the peace of His truth instead of being overwhelmed by fear. But it was hard, and I felt as if I failed as often as I succeeded.

When you feel frightened, discouraged, or abandoned, do the words of Deuteronomy 31:8 bring you peace or do they sound hollow?

_____

_____

_____

_____

The truth is that God will never give you more than you and God can handle together.

It's hard to keep the faith when everything around us seems to be going downhill fast. Friends and acquaintances don't help with some of their well-meaning comments, do they? How often do you hear, "God will never give you more than you can handle"?

Of course, God will give you more than you can handle—that's how faith is grown! You wouldn't need Him if you could handle everything by yourself. You wouldn't turn to Him if you had all the resources you needed to make it through the storm on your own. Satan wants us to believe we can face the storm in our own strength. When we try, and we fail, he'll tell us God left us to face the storm alone because He doesn't love us.

The truth is that God will never give you more than you and God can handle *together*. Scripture tells us that, without Christ, we can do nothing (John 15:5) but that, with God, all things are possible (Matthew 19:26; Ephesians 3:20). Yes, all things are possible but, as we already know, when the storm howls through our lives, not all things are given when or how we ask. We must face each day, arm-in-arm with God, drawing on His strength, wisdom, and comfort. As we learn more about Him, Jesus stretches our faith.

If you read those words and think, "I don't want my faith stretched; it fits perfectly just the size it is!"—I have terrible news: That's too bad! God has several purposes in stretching your faith. One is to move you off the baby food of spiritual teaching and onto real meat. Another is beautifully expressed in 2 Corinthians 4:6–10, where Paul says God has given you the glorious Light of the Holy Spirit; so when life beats you up, you must see it as an opportunity to live out the life of Jesus before others.

I know . . . that doesn't make me want to throw a party, either. But Jesus took the pain of my sin when He died—the least I can do is live for Him when I'm suffering.

 How has God become more real to you as you've walked through difficult times? How has He stretched your faith?

_____

_____

_____

_____

A Whale of a Story
During a time I was struggling with my circumstances, the Lord led me to the book of Jonah, someone who was definitely in the center of a storm (Jonah 1). When we're reading this story, we learn that Jonah caused his suffering by his stubborn disobedience. I've had some trying times when I refused to obey God; I'm sure you have, too. This isn't always the cause of our storms, but the lessons God taught me in Jonah have universal application.

As we read in Jonah, we find the Lord gave him a job to do—a job Jonah didn't want to do. So he went down to the nearest seaport and jumped aboard a ship, thinking he could sail away to where the Lord couldn't find him. I've never jumped on a ship, but I've tried ignoring God. That doesn't work, either.

Once the ship was at sea, God brought on a terrible storm, almost destroying the ship. The sailors soon discovered Jonah was the cause of the storm. Jonah confessed his sin and suggested that the only way to save the ship and the sailor's lives was to throw him overboard. Reluctantly, the sailors agreed to throw him into the violent sea. Both the sailors and Jonah believed he was sentenced to death. As soon as he was thrown overboard, the sea became calm.

I remember when things in my life were going from bad to worse, just as they seemed to be for Jonah. I stood in my living room, my face defiant in anger and my fists clinched. I yelled at God, "I am going to find a different god to handle this mess because You aren't doing anything right!" It wasn't long before I was on my face before Him, broken-hearted. There is no other God! *"I am the first and I am the last; apart from me there is no God"* (Isaiah 44:6b).

Praise His holy name, the Lord who created the universe held me until I calmed down enough to be teachable! Then my Father God took me back to Jonah to give me a few sustaining truths from this wonderful account. These lifelines were essential to me as I struggled and crawled through difficulties and times of suffering in my own life. Without these lifesavers, I would've perished in the storm. God may minister to you during the height of the storm in different ways, but perhaps, when the deluge rages, He'll use these lifelines to guide you to the spiritual bread and water essential to your faith. I pray these sweet truths will feed your hungry soul and restore your hope.

KEEP TALKING TO GOD

Jonah was a prophet, called by God to carry His words to His people. But now, as he faced death in the vast sea, it was a little late for obedience. Because Jonah knew his desperate plight was his own fault, dare he pray? Could he pray with panic surging through his body? But Jonah knew his Lord was One of grace and mercy—the One who still looks upon you and me with grace and mercy (Hebrews 4:16)!

> *"In my distress I called to the LORD, and he answered me. From the depths of the grave I called for help, and you listened to my cry."*
> (Jonah 2:2)

When Jonah uttered this prayer, he was drowning in the sea. Waves swept over him and seaweed was wrapped around his head (Jonah 2:3, 5). Even in this hopeless circumstance, he knew if he cried out to God, God would respond (Psalm 102:17–20). Jonah prayed, and his God answered!

When you are drowning, communication with your Father is so essential.

When you are drowning, communication with your Father is so essential. If all you can do is cry—cry. If all you can do is yell at Him—yell. When you're communicating with Him, your mind and thoughts are toward Him and He can minister to you, speak to you, and comfort you. If you shut Him out, He can't reach you. Just when you might least want to talk to your Father, that's when it's most important you do. When it's hardest for you to hear His voice, that's when His words are most critical. How can you hear His gentle whisper when your mind's scattered in a million directions and pushed to the edge of exhaustion (1 Kings 19:11, 12)?

I understand what it feels like, reading words of Scripture that have always spoken comfort to you, only to find they just rattle around in your brain—or worse, sound hollow. Express your emotions and needs to your Father and you'll receive His comfort, strength, and wisdom in return (Psalm 119:50, 107; John 6:63). Hold on to Jesus—you will hear, you will see, you will speak again (Luke 7:22).

If all you want do is yell at Him in anger and frustration, bring it on! He can take it. Rest assured, you can't say anything He hasn't heard before. I've said it all! And before us, Job, David, and a host of others said it all (Job 10:1–7; 30:20–23; Psalms 13:1, 2; 22:1, 2). Jesus died to give you the confidence to approach God with complete honesty (Psalm 62:8; Ephesians 3:12). My philosophy is that He knows my thoughts anyway (Psalm 139:2); I might as well get them out in the open where He can help me deal with them. And believe me, He will deal with each and every emotion you express. If you're honest, He'll reveal Himself to you. He'll get to the heart of every emotion and teach you about yourself. When the yelling's done, not only will you be changed, but your relationship with Him will be richer.

What emotion do you want to express to your Father, from either a past or present trial?

_____

_____

_____

Perhaps you're so exhausted no words will come. That's okay! Rest in the promise that He knows exactly where you are and what you need, without you uttering a word (Psalm 139:4; Isaiah 65:24). He's the One who's with you in every trial and sees your every need. Sometimes, when I shut my eyes to pray, I only hear chaos and confusion. I remember a time when I allowed the mayhem to rob me of peace and sleep. I tossed and turned, feeling a void where my connection to God had been. Then a friend reminded me of Romans 8:26, 27, which promises that the Holy Spirit prays for us when we can't pray.

That night I climbed in bed with an old, softbound Bible I'd had since a teenager. I hugged it to my chest and whispered to my Father, "I'm too drained to pray, but I'll lie here and listen while the Spirit prays for me." After lying in silence for a few minutes, I drifted off to sleep and had the first full night's rest I'd had in months. This became my nightly ritual, and peace began to return to my waking hours. My circumstances didn't change, but what a powerful Prayer Partner I had! After a few months of intercession by the Holy Spirit, I found my voice in prayer again.

Sleeping with me was hard on that old Bible, though, and after a few months it began to fall apart. My husband and I went shopping for a new one and I'm sure you can imagine his embarrassment when I had to "hug check" each one to make sure I found a suitable replacement. If you can't gather your thoughts to pray, stand on the promise the Holy Spirit is praying for you. Find a few minutes during the day when you can sit quietly, letting Him speak for you.

During this time, when praying is not easy for you, that doesn't mean it should go undone. This is a great time to call in the reserves. Enlist a few close friends with whom you can talk safely each day, without worrying about the rumor mill. Praying for you will be such a blessed ministry for them (James 5:16; 1 Thessalonians 5:11). Share the events of the day with them so they can pray specifically for you. Vague prayer requests leave you, and them, unable to see God's answers. Seeing His answers will grow all of you spiritually. When you're able to pray again, you must also pray specifically. Clearly tell God what you need and want Him to do, but take care not to confuse who's God and who's the servant. There's a great difference between expressing what you want and commanding God to do what you want, when you want it. Praying specifically allows you to rejoice when you see His work in your life; praying submissively allows you to see His sovereignty in your life.

> *Praying specifically allows you to rejoice when you see God's work in your life; praying submissively allows you to see His sovereignty in your life.*

 I encourage you to choose a verse reminding you how critical it is to stay in touch with your Lord during your stormy days (Psalm 91:15). Choose one I've referenced or an old favorite. Write out your choice below and also on the Faith Focus card under the title "Prayer."

_____

_____

_____

GOD HAS A PLAN

Does your storm seem to be getting worse day by day? In this lies your hope: God has a plan. I know you can't feel it. I know you can't see it. Do you think Jonah could? Being thrown overboard to die at sea didn't seem like a step in the right direction. But Jonah didn't die, because God had a plan for him. Jonah *couldn't* die. He hadn't done the job God told him to do!

> *"But the* LORD *provided a great fish to swallow Jonah, and Jonah was inside the fish three days and three nights."* (Jonah 1:17)

I've heard this great fish called a whale since childhood, so I'll continue the tradition. The Lord sent a whale to swallow Jonah. Now, at first, we might not see being swallowed by a whale as an improvement in Jonah's situation, but let's recall a few facts: The ship was at sea, miles from nowhere, with no nice beaches or resort islands in sight; we have no proof Jonah could swim, and even if he could, he couldn't swim for days with no food or fresh water; no rescuers were coming to save him, because the seamen who threw him overboard thought he was dead (Jonah 1:14). I think we can safely say, Jonah was in a hopeless situation. But then, along came this deliverer whale. Certainly not what Jonah had in mind, but it worked.

You probably haven't been swallowed by a whale lately, but I'm sure you've watched as a turn of events during a crisis only made matters worse. The storm was at its peak, yet the sky grew darker, troubles thundered louder, and bad news rained down even harder. Your prayers just hit the ceiling and slapped you back in the face. I've certainly had a prayer or two slap me.

Once, while we struggled to scrape together money for extensive roof repairs after a bad storm (appraised at just under our insurance deductible, of course), the sewer line in our backyard decided it was a great time to rupture. That was way beyond my husband's handyman skills, so we called three companies for bids. The bids weren't even in yet when our car broke down and had to be towed to the shop. We were faced with three sizeable bills, one right after another, and we didn't have the money for the first one! What made it even more exciting was that the chemical plant at which my husband worked had just been sold, and the purchasing company had not yet released the very short list of current employees who would be retained. Three big bills and the probability that my husband would be laid off. Believe me, I questioned God's planning skills. Perhaps Jonah had some questions, too.

Have you ever been or are you now in a situation that seems hopeless? What questions did you ask (or are you asking) God?

_____

_____

_____

_____

Cling to this unshakable truth: Your Father God is mighty in power and in control of every moment; nothing is beyond His might (Jeremiah 32:17).

Your Father God is mighty in power and in control of every moment; nothing is beyond His might.

Remember, He's with you and He'll comfort you. He sustains your every breath and hears your every sob (Psalm 55:22; Isaiah 46:4). You might not understand the twists and turns the path takes as you stumble along. Understanding might not come until you kneel before His throne in Heaven, but you are surrounded by Him now (Psalm 125:1, 2).

Though your questions may remain unanswered, God has heard you and will use your seeking to increase your faith. He never leaves you, and every day furthers His plans to complete His purpose in you (Jeremiah 29:11). God's plans are perfect and they never fail (Deuteronomy 32:3, 4; Isaiah 14:24). Place your trust in the One who is never surprised by events; the One who never sleeps (Psalm 121:3, 4). Your Father is upholding you with His mighty right hand (Isaiah 41:10).

Before Jonah was born, God knew it would take three days in a whale to get him to obey when God called him. And you thought you were stubborn! Before you were born, God had planned every day of your life (Psalm 139:14–16). His name is *I AM*—not I WAS or I MIGHT BE (Exodus 3:14)! He moves above time, and all your tomorrows are known to Him. You can trust His sovereignty. His wisdom is perfect and His knowledge is unfathomable (Psalm 147:5, Isaiah 40:28). You can trust His love. He carries you tenderly in His arms as a shepherd carries a beloved lamb (Isaiah 40:11).

 Choose a verse that affirms to your heart God's control, either from the ones I've referenced or a favorite you have in mind. Write out your choice below and also on the Faith Focus card under the title "Sovereignty."

_____

_____

_____

_____

Before we move on, let me tell you how God resolved the string of expenses I described earlier. While I was praying (translation: griping), when the car was still in the shop, a quiet thought came to me: God owns the cattle on a thousand hills. I tried to ignore the thought but it grew louder: God owns the cattle on a thousand hills. I recognized it as being from His Word and found it to be from Psalm 50:10. I remarked that, if He owned all those cows, He could sell three of them for me so I could pay my bills.

When Charlie came home from work that evening, I told him about the little sparring during my prayer time. He looked at me as though I'd lost my mind (a common occurrence), but said nothing. Later that evening, he said, "The company I used to work for has decided to give me an end-of-the-year bonus. Even though I don't currently work for them, I was with them eleven months of the past year, so they want me to have it."

I looked at Him in amazement and shrieked, "That's Cow #1!" Even more amazing, Charlie was one of only a few original employees retained by the new company, and they were all given a sign-on bonus a few days later: Cow #2! A month later Cow #3 (a third unexpected sum of money) arrived, and it paid the remaining bill. Three unexpected bills, three sums of money providing what we needed. With my attitude, God should've left me to

God carries you tenderly in His arms as a shepherd carries a beloved lamb.

> *"The Lord is not slow in keeping his promise, as some understand slowness. He is patient with you, not wanting anyone to perish, but everyone to come to repentance."*
>
> *2 Peter 3:9*

struggle and penny-pinch, but He chose to deliver me in a way that demonstrated His planning of these details in my life (Psalm 50:15). My only response can be, *"You are awesome, O God"* (Psalm 68:35)!

God doesn't often choose to deliver us in such a wonderful way. The hardest thing to remember is that we are earth-sighted, while God is eternity-sighted. All we know of life is what we've experienced since we took our first wailing breath. God has a perfect plan for your life. His plan centers around the most important decision you will ever make while on this earth—and it's not what career you'll have or who you'll marry. Everything about your life is designed to show you that you need Jesus as your Savior and to give you an opportunity to accept Him (2 Peter 3:9).

I had the wonderful blessing of working for three years with the crew of the Space Shuttle Columbia mission, which ended in 2003 with the loss of the Columbia orbiter and the lives of the seven precious crewmembers on board. Because I knew the crewmembers well, their loss was devastating to me. While preparing for that mission, the launch date was delayed many times, causing great frustration for the crewmembers and for those of us working the mission. There was great joy when that shuttle finally launched, followed by unspeakable heartache sixteen days later. As you can imagine, many poured their hearts out to God in grief, not understanding why seven wonderful lives had to be lost.

A few weeks following the tragedy, God brought me to 2 Peter 3:9, assuring me His hand had been upon the mission from the very first day of planning. Every launch delay was His grace, giving each unbelieving crewmember an additional opportunity to meet His Son Jesus. Month after month, for two years after the original launch date, the delays piled up. God's grace covered the mission because He knew its outcome before it even began.

If you do not know Jesus as your Savior, God has planned your life with event after event full of grace. Accept Him now, because there will come a time when He will hear your no for the last time and the opportunities will end. Jesus is the only answer to your heart-questions, the only way to true inner peace. I will not lie to you. If you accept Jesus, the rest of your life will be spent in God's hands, while you are being molded into the image of His Son (Romans 8:29). As a believer, your earthly life won't be easy, because He'll be fashioning you for an eternal kingdom and to prosper you in eternity (Isaiah 64:8; Matthew 25:34).

APPLY Choose a verse I've referenced or a favorite you already have and write it below and on your Faith Focus card under the title "God's Plan."

_____

_____

_____

_____

LOOKING UP

Exhaustion, isolation, depression—these are the shackles of suffering. They weigh us down and keep us from looking up to God from the midst of the storm. Our chains can be broken by an attitude of praise and the strength we gain from our Christian family. Praise? That seems impossible! Who wants to praise God for our pain? Even so, praise and the strength of those around us enable us to lift our eyes to God.

Praise under Pressure

Every word of Jonah's prayer echoed praise. Even in his disobedience, he experienced God's grace. He praised God for answered prayer, even though his circumstances hadn't changed (Jonah 2:2). He praised God for deliverance, even though he was still buried in the belly of the whale (Jonah 2:6b). His heart was filled with the hope of praise and thanksgiving, even though all seemed hopeless (Jonah 2:4, 9). As Jonah praised God, his eyes were lifted beyond his circumstances to faith in God.

God inhabits praise! He'll rise up within you when you praise Him. No matter how you feel, your soul will take baby steps toward joy and strength as words of praise tumble from your lips. I know, you won't feel like it when you start, but with every word you'll feel a little better. Praise lifts your heart and fills your soul with the certainty He's with you to bring His light and love into your darkest moments.

  How has praise revealed the light of God's presence even though you felt trapped in darkness?

_____

_____

_____

During one of my darkest moments, my Father led me to a beautiful verse that's a treasure to me: *"Splendor and majesty are before him; strength and joy in his dwelling place"* (1 Chronicles 16:27). As I prayed about these words, a powerful truth was revealed to me. Every believer is God's temple because of the indwelling of the Holy Spirit (1 Corinthians 3:16). I'm His dwelling place. You're His dwelling place. If strength and joy are in His dwelling place, then strength and joy are in you and me—whether we feel them or not! How many hours have I spent before God, asking Him to give me His strength, and then walking away, thinking He hadn't heard me because I did not *feel* any different? Feelings do not convey truth; His Word conveys truth. When we praise Him, He brings our feelings in line with the truth: His strength, joy, power, and majesty—all He is dwells within us. When you praise Him, the Holy Spirit within you rises up to join in and it's impossible for your soul not to respond with renewed life.

When you praise the Lord, even as tears are wetting your cheeks with sorrow, not only does the light of joy begin to dawn in your soul, but the pain in your heart will lessen just a little. Praise softens your heart and allows your desire to be with Him to grow. You'll hunger for His presence and thirst for His Word.

Feelings do not convey truth; God's Word conveys truth.

God is always with you—praise enables you to be with Him.

Praise turns you on to Jesus! You spiritual nerves wake up and you become aware of His presence. Your face lifts toward Heaven instead of studying the dirt on the floor. His Word ministers to you instead of lying dry in your heart. Tears will still fall, but they'll be healing tears. God is always with you—praise enables you to be with Him.

Words of praise open the windows of your memory, allowing you to recall the Rock that God has been in your life. As you look back He's always been there. He's been your Comforter, your Guide, your Father. He's never failed you nor forsaken you. There have been joyful times over the years, many that you can see were brought about by His hand. Camp in those memories for a while. Allow God to comfort you with the joys and victories you've experienced with Him. Graduation? Your first job? A special moment shared with someone dear to you? The birth of your child or a child precious to you? A great promotion at work? A restoring vacation? A close parking spot when it's raining? Any or all of these?

APPLY What joys and victories come to mind when you look back over your life?

_____

_____

_____

_____

Thanksgiving in the Trenches

> *"But I, with a song of thanksgiving, will sacrifice to you."* (Jonah 2:9a)

It seems strange to be thankful from the belly of a whale, doesn't it? As Jonah praised God for the grace given to him in the present, he was able to thank Him for the assurance of deliverance tomorrow.

Jonah's words expressed the promise that he would bring God a song of thanksgiving when he got out of the whale. You, too, might be willing to sing all the thanksgiving songs you can muster—after the storm has blown over. Unfortunately, that won't be much help in the midst of the storm. When you praise God for His work in your life yesterday, you'll be able to thank Him for His hand in the storm today. Words of thanksgiving fill you with faith for the future.

I can hear you now: "How can I be grateful when I'm being tossed about by this storm like a toothpick in a tempest?" Am I saying to leap up right now and thank God profusely for the agony you are going through? Well, Paul says we should, but I'll never be Paul, so let's just settle for some baby steps, okay? Ask God to show you every single day something positive for which you can be thankful, no matter how small. Expect something. Watch for it. Revel in it. A favorite song on the radio, a flower by the side of the road, a snowflake, a child's smile in the checkout line, your dog turning inside out with joy at the door when you get home—you'll find many blessings to be thankful for each day if you're looking through "gratitude eyes." Then, as you lie in bed each night, recount in a prayer of thanksgiving the blessings God rained down on you—instead of griping at Him because you had to brave the storm for yet another day. Going to sleep with blessings running through your head makes for a much softer pillow than grumbles do.

APPLY During troubled times, what verse from God's Word lifts your heart to praise and thanksgiving? Record it here and on your Faith Focus card under the title "Praise."

_____

_____

_____

_____

Strength in Numbers

While an attitude of praise and thanksgiving might be hard to manage when you're cowering alone in the corner with the wind whipping around you, worshipping with other believers can fill your soul with joy. Songs of praise minister to your heart, and hymns of thanksgiving turn your thoughts to gratitude. In so many ways, God uses your sisters in Christ to strengthen you and bring your eyes back to Jesus. Alone, the dangers of despair are very real; surrounded by the family of God, our fear becomes faith.

Have you ever watched a nature show in which the lion is hunting for his lunch? He'll approach a herd of antelope or another tasty beast, and soon, the herd catches wind of him and begins to run. The lion holds back, cleverly watching for a weak member of the herd to fall behind and become separated from the main group. When the weak one is alone, the lion attacks. Kind of smart on the lion's part, huh? He doesn't attack the whole herd and fight them off, trying to pull one out of the center of the group. I don't think the wording describing Satan in 1 Peter 5:8b is an accident: _"Your enemy the devil prowls around like a roaring lion looking for someone to devour."_

The Enemy knows when we are weak. When hardship or suffering comes, he attacks us like a roaring lion, hoping the weak one will separate from the church, the body of Christ (Romans 8:38, 39; 1 Corinthians 3:23). He knows, if he can get us off on our own, we'll be much more vulnerable. We'll be less able to resist his whispered lies and his temptations. How often do we play into his hands? Perhaps we keep going to church at first, but then we begin to fear that everyone is tired of seeing our sad faces and hearing our sad story, so we make excuses and stay home. At first we may stay home because emotions are overwhelming; then, before we know it, we are home every Sunday.

You need to stay in Bible study so your mind will be alert and recognize Satan's lies when he tries to deceive you. You need to be in worship, drinking in the words sung by your church family, even if your heart is so heavy you can't sing yourself (Hebrews 10:25). Let their voices minister to your soul. Corporate worship will bring your eyes to Jesus when you can't find Him on your own (Psalms 95:1, 2; 105:1-4; 111:1; 122:1).

If you have withdrawn from the church or fellow believers when going through hardship, how did that make the path more difficult? If you've turned to your church family during these times, how has their love and support helped you?

_____

_____

_____

_____

Corporate worship will bring our eyes to Jesus when you can't find Him on your own.

> **To know you're being prayed for brings a peace to your heart that's indescribable.**

As a woman going through difficulty or tragedy, there's no time when you need your sisters in Christ more! It's important you be as open with them as you can comfortably be, and let them surround you with the tenderness only women can give. They will uplift you by pouring their encouragement and strength into you. Consider the close friends you have, the ones you tend to turn to first when you've had a bad day or when difficulty strikes. Do they pray with you and encourage you? Do they strengthen you by reminding you of God's Word? Do they help you lift your eyes toward Jesus—or jump on the negative bandwagon with you?

Above all, draw on the strength and prayers of your friends and family. Nothing soothes like the honest and heartfelt prayers spoken over you by those who love you. Ask them to put your name and a brief description of your needs on their prayer chains. This will flood God's throne room with thousands of voices interceding on your behalf (Nehemiah 4:9). Ask God to make you aware of the blessing of intercession. To know you're being prayed for brings a peace to your heart that's indescribable. And for those who have the blessing of praying for you? What joy they receive from the opportunity to serve God and to obey His command to *"carry each other's burdens"* (Galatians 6:2; also see Ephesians 6:18)! Allow others to serve God by ministering to you.

APPLY Can you describe a time you knew you were being prayed for and tell how it strengthened you?

_____

_____

_____

_____

Write a verse below that strengthens you when difficult times come. Copy it on your Faith Focus card under the title "Strength."

_____

_____

_____

_____

One Step at a Time

STAND ON GOD'S TRUTH

One afternoon, I stood by a loved one, anxiously awaiting the verdict in a jury trial. My loved one was completely innocent of the charges and I knew God would not—could not—allow the lies to win. In the instant it took the jury foreman to say the word, "Guilty!" my image of God was shattered. How could He allow an innocent person's life to be destroyed? How could He allow truth to be defeated?

Do you know what it's like to feel as though everything you've based your life on has melted around your feet? As the dark weeks passed after that day in the courtroom, my emotions were raw. I found it too hard to think about next week, or even tomorrow—I just tried to make it through the next hour. My emotions and my thoughts told me nothing was certain anymore; yet, deep in my mind, there was an assurance that God's truth never changes (Isaiah 40:8). I struggled to rebuild the foundation I felt had been ripped from beneath my feet.

Nothing is as critical to our troubled lives as God's Word. I kept repeating His truths to myself every waking moment. God's truth is the foundation on which I crawl or stand, and it gave me strength every day. I was all too aware of Satan's schemes. He continually stood beside me to accuse me (Zechariah 3:1). Hallelujah, the Lord is forever rebuking him and claiming me as His own (Zechariah 3:2)! But if I allowed myself to forget that truth, I panicked and listened to Satan's voice. Slowly, after days of willing myself to repeat what I knew to be true, my thoughts and emotions began to recover from the quicksand of uncertainty and to find the solid footing of God's truth.

Satan's desire is to steal God's truth from you and replace it with his lies (Mark 4:15). Allow the Holy Spirit to bring God's Word continually to your mind so your thoughts are controlled by truth and not open to Satan's deceit (John 16:13). Satan is the father of lies (John 8:44) and when you listen to him, it only leads to confusion and hopelessness.

But when the days are terribly dark, Satan's voice is so tempting! It's so silky smooth and he says just what you want to hear. He is the most treacherous of liars! He desires not to lead you out of your suffering, but to lead you into bondage—bondage to despair. He desires for you to become despondent and defeated. He'll whisper to you that each day is going to be worse than the day before. He'll fill your mind with fear and dread until a downward spiral becomes your expectation. Even if a positive change happens in your situation, you'll be too blinded by hopelessness to notice it. "My life stinks!" is not a mantra that results in hope for the future!

Whose voice are you listening to right now, when you try to reconcile the scars of your suffering with the truth of God's love? Do you truly believe the truth of Jesus Christ is more powerful than the lies of Satan? Are you ready to choose God's truth over the lies?

How has God healed your wounds during times of suffering?

_____

_____

_____

_____

> **When we focus on God's truths they lift our spirits; He is the Father of peace, not doubt and confusion.**

When we focus on God's truths they lift our spirits; He is the Father of peace, not doubt and confusion (1 Corinthians 14:33a). Even during suffering, an underlying bedrock of peace and joy will allow you to feel hope. God's Word is Truth: timeless, changeless, a Light for your heart and soul when all else is in darkness (Isaiah 40:8; Mark 13:31; 1 John 1:5b). Truth is not a whim that blows in the wind. Truth is the person of Jesus Christ, who loves you so much He died for you and is now seated in Heaven, interceding for and ministering to you. Truth will not mold itself to your or any other person's passing fancy. It stands on the Rock of God's character and is expressed in every promise spoken by His faithfulness. God is the Father of peace, joy, strength, wisdom, hope, and so much more. Focus on Him! Let His Word become your Bread of Life and your Living Water to sustain you in the wilderness of suffering.

What are these truths? We have seen many of them before, but they are important enough for you to allow them to wash over your soul again.

"How great is the love the Father has lavished on us, that we should be called children of God!" (1 John 3:1)

"If we confess our sins, he is faithful and just and will forgive us our sins and purify us from all unrighteousness." (1 John 1:9)

"The one who is in you is greater than the one who is in the world." (1 John 4:4b)

"For God did not give us a spirit of timidity, but a spirit of power, of love and of self-discipline." (2 Timothy 1:7)

"For the eyes of the Lord are on the righteous and his ears are attentive to their prayer." (1 Peter 3:12)

"But now, this is what the LORD says—he who created you, O Jacob, he who formed you, O Israel: 'Fear not, for I have redeemed you; I have summoned you by name; you are mine. When you pass through the waters, I will be with you; and when you pass through the rivers, they will not sweep over you. When you walk through the fire, you will not be burned; the flames will not set you ablaze.'" (Isaiah 43:1, 2)

"The eternal God is your refuge, and underneath are the everlasting arms." (Deuteronomy 33:27a)

"As for God, his way is perfect; the word of the LORD is flawless. He is a shield for all who take refuge in him." (2 Samuel 22:31)

"Come to me, all you who are weary and burdened, and I will give you rest." (Matthew 11:28)

"Your word is a lamp to my feet and a light for my path." (Psalm 119:105)

God's Truth is always victorious— if we bring it to the fight.

APPLY So many wonderful promises fill God's Word, available to you to encourage and strengthen you. Pick one to write here and to record on your Faith Focus card under the title "Encouragement."

_____

_____

_____

_____

These promises and so many more we've learned as we've come through this study are ours to stuff in our minds and hearts until they are so full Satan's lies cannot penetrate at all! On this earth, truth does not always defeat lies; but in our minds and hearts, where battles in the spiritual realm are fought, God's Truth is always victorious—if we bring it to the fight. I don't understand suffering but I know my God is a God of purpose. I don't understand the battles we must fight, but I do know He never allows us to be defeated or destroyed. He's always with us, upholding us with His hand. He never forsakes us and He preserves us forever. Walk with Him, dear one, one step at a time.

Precious ladies, how I pray you have reached this point feeling encouraged and uplifted, knowing there are others who have stumbled down the same path you have, and have slept many nights on a similar pillow, damp with tears. Your sweet Jesus has been there, too. He has stumbled; He has cried. Now He stands, bearing the scars of His suffering, wanting more than anything to strengthen you and comfort you as you face your struggles. It is your choice whether you will listen to His voice. It is your choice whether you will trust Him.

I know how hard it is! Just as I was finishing this chapter, my dear mother-in-law suddenly became ill. Because of my own mother's death, I greatly overreacted. I panicked, becoming very upset. I told God I couldn't handle another illness of a dear mother and He'd better do something fast! I was an emotional wreck and all the wonderful words written in these six chapters went right down the drain! After everything calmed down and my mother-in-law was safe and sound, I realized I had failed the test miserably. I decided I would just stop writing this book, then and there! I felt like a hypocrite and refused to write about what I obviously couldn't do.

My indispensable Prayer Partner reminded me, in no uncertain terms, that I am a weak, fallible human being and I will never be able to get this faith thing down perfect. Every crisis and every bad day find me going back to these chapters to remind myself how I'm supposed to respond. Maybe you will do better. I pray that this study will be a good resource to grab when the next cloud peeks over the horizon. I don't understand why God chose me to write this—I guess He had to use someone! I don't understand why life is this way, but I do know my Jesus. Nothing else in this world is certain. He is not only *how* I live, He is *why* I live.

Hard choices are ahead. Spend a quiet few minutes with your Savior and Lord. Write a prayer to Him, honestly expressing your desire to follow and trust Him during the storm. Be honest about your fears and doubts. Give them to Him. He's the Author of your faith; let Him write the solution.

_____

_____

_____

_____

_____

_____

_____

_____

_____

_____

Notes

7

It Came to Pass

I titled this chapter "It Came to Pass" because it's my favorite phrase from God's Word. You see it all the time: *"It came to pass, when . . ."* or *"It came to pass, in the time of . . ."* Now, I admit, I'm not using the phrase in that way; I'm gleefully pulling it out of context. When I say, "It came to pass," I mean, "it came so it could pass," as in "go away"!

Any storm, no matter how dark, will end. No matter how long it has parked in your life, it will move on! Your Father, who's walked with you in the darkness, will now help you to heal your broken spirit and to put the pieces of your life back together—if you allow Him to. Let me say that again: *if* you allow Him to. You may have no control over the advancing storm or over the outcome that shattered your life—but you do have control over the person you become as you walk out the other side.

As the storm clouds disappear or as you reflect on burdens you carry from past trials, now is the time you must make choices. God's power to renew you will be released in your life based on the choices you make in the weeks and months to come. It won't be easy—you can't make these choices on your own, but God will perfectly match His strengths with your weaknesses (2 Corinthians 13:9). Let's consider these questions:

- Do you want to come out of a time of suffering with a faith that is growing stronger?

- Do you want to be spiritually victorious in difficult circumstances?
- Do you want to look back, in months and years to come, and see how God revealed Himself through the storms you've experienced?

If the answer to these questions is yes, come with me as we make these choices together.

"For our light and momentary troubles are achieving for us an eternal glory that far outweighs them all."

2 Corinthians 4:17

CHOOSE TO CHOOSE!

"Look at the nations and watch—and be utterly amazed. For I am going to do something in your days that you would not believe, even if you were told." (Habakkuk 1:5)

Do you have a favorite Scripture verse? I do: Habakkuk 1:5. Years ago, I didn't even know the book of Habakkuk existed—I'm still not sure how to pronounce it! A dear friend who helped me during a difficult time led me to it. The prophet Habakkuk complained to God as he watched good, decent people who loved the Lord live hard lives full of suffering, while those who ignored God lived a life of roses. The world hasn't changed much, has it? The Lord answered Habakkuk by showing him the ultimate fate of evil men. When he understood that the Lord would destroy evildoers and save His people to an eternity with Him, he realized the same truth the apostle Paul would later express: This life of hardship is incredibly brief compared with the eternity of joy we're promised with God (Romans 8:18; 2 Corinthians 4:17).

Couldn't we all use Habakkuk 1:5 spoken into our lives? Wouldn't you love it if the Lord came to you and said:

Look at _____ and watch—and be utterly amazed. For I am going to do something in your circumstance that you would not believe, even if you were told. (Author's paraphrase)

 Look at the blank in the verse above. If God could reach into one of your difficult events from the past, or a storm you're experiencing today, what would you write in that blank?

_____

_____

_____

As you look at what you've written, I hope you know you have the right as God's child to pray continually for your request—until He specifically says no or closes the door by your circumstances (Philippians 4:6). Continue to ask until He's blessed you with a response (Genesis 32:26). If He has said no—let it go. Don't bring it up again, don't whine about it, don't use it as an excuse when you disobey Him. If He's refused you, it's because He knew a different action is best for your earthly or eternal life. Choose to trust Him.

Storms leave spiritual scars, no matter how they are resolved. A time of suffering leaves wounds that need to be healed. Faith and doubt mingle in your heart. If the crisis ends with your world in shambles, not only must you heal from the impact of the storm, you must also learn to live with the outcome, which might echo for years to come. Your Father waits to do the hard work required to heal your wounds, but you must choose to surrender to His touch.

When I lost my sweet Mom, a part of my life changed forever. Gone were the daily phone calls, the special times we spent together, and the excitement of sharing those "Mom-things" with her. As the years passed by, I slowly surrendered this pain to my Father and He comforted and healed my heart. Although no one will ever replace my precious Mom, He's led me to special friendships that provide some of the treasures of the relationship I shared with her.

If your life's been forever changed by a time of suffering, what pain are you holding tight to your heart instead of surrendering to your Father?

_____

_____

_____

_____

To surrender my pain was a conscious choice on my part. As the storm passes, you'll face many choices. Your heavenly Father desires to re-create your world and Jesus desires to heal you from within (2 Corinthians 5:17). Will you emerge a stronger woman of faith, with a knowledge of God greater than when the hard days began? Or will you choose to carry sadness, anger, or bitterness within you for years to come? Allow your Father to comfort and heal you (2 Corinthians 1:3).

If you leave these wounds open, they'll become weapons in Satan's hands. He'll use past sadness to rob you of the joy your Father wants to give you now. He'll use festering anger to destroy new relationships your Father wants to bring to you now. He'll use lingering bitterness to hinder new personal and spiritual growth God wants you to experience now. Your Father is the Lord of the past, present, and future (Revelation 1:8). Choose to surrender the past to Him so He can bless you today and tomorrow.

When I was young, I was deeply hurt by another person's sin. Through the years, I've struggled with the fact that God didn't intervene to stop him. Although God has used this experience to allow me to minister to many who have had a similar heartache, the humiliation of that difficult time occasionally rears its ugly head. I'm afraid I've not yet allowed God to fully heal that wound. I choose to carry this old baggage with me, convincing myself it's protection, that it keeps me from being so vulnerable and open to pain again. In reality, this is only Satan's lie—a lie that keeps me from enjoying the richness of relationships God has for me.

What baggage from a past storm are you carrying that hinders your personal and spiritual growth and prevents you from living the abundant life Jesus longs to give you (John 10:10)?

_____

_____

_____

_____

Your heavenly Father desires to re-create your world and Jesus desires to heal you from within.

Don't allow pain and anger from your past to define who you are today.

No good comes from old baggage; it is only a heavy burden, dragging you down. It's time to choose between the old and the new. Don't allow pain and anger from your past to define who you are today. No matter how painful your wastelands are, He can transform them into a beautiful garden (Isaiah 51:3); no matter how dry you feel, He can turn your life into a refreshing pool of water (Isaiah 41:18). Come with me as we set our baggage down at the throne of our Father and *leave it there*. As you walk away, feel the tension leaving your body. Feel strained emotions relaxing. Watch the silver lining on those clouds expanding to fill the whole sky as the clouds melt away.

So many choices lie ahead. Will we struggle with every twist and turn of our circumstances or choose to be at rest in God's sovereignty? Are we determined to be haunted by the blame we place on others and ourselves or will we ask God to teach us of His love and provision during the storm? Do we keep our hearts buried in the pain of the past or allow God to bring us into a new life of hope?

APPLY As you consider the choices that face you, which one might be the hardest for you to make?

_____

_____

_____

_____

Why am I determined to be critical rather than contented? I'm so busy complaining, I forget to praise God for His presence and thank Him for His provision. And old baggage? I haul my bags around like gold medals and refuse to leave them at God's throne so I can step into the future He's prepared for me.

The choices ahead of us are hard to make—they take work. How often do we choose the easy but destructive path and avoid the effort required to let God heal us? Self-pity is easier than surrender. Turn your face toward God and allow Him to guide you through the choices that will bring you freedom.

It Came to Pass

DAY TWO

God will pick up the pieces of your life and use them to build a faith stronger than it ever was before.

CHOOSE TO MOVE

There are times when God's sovereignty hurts. The storm may pass into the distance but the journey is painful. You look in the mirror—what do you see? A face strained by exhaustion and fractured nerves. Boy, have I been there! You wonder, "How can I change from the wreck I am now into a woman with stronger faith and a renewed spirit? How can I ever trust God again?" Praise God—you don't have to change by yourself! God is waiting to help you. He'll pick up the pieces of your life and use them to build a faith stronger than it ever was before. He waits to reveal Himself to you from within the experiences you've endured. All He requires from you is surrender.

Did I say "all"?! It won't be easy; you must surrender your desire for things to be different. You must surrender your desire to have a pity party. Oh, how I hate to give that up! No one loves a pity party as much as I do. I buy a new dress, invite all my friends, and we go through boxes and boxes of tissues! But God can't heal you when you're hidden behind a wall of pity. Surrender it all: your exhaustion, your self-pity, your lack of faith, even your distrust—He'll transform these into a strong faith that will carry you into (and through) every tomorrow.

The answer, dear one, is to *choose* to move! Whisper to Him, "I don't want to stay where I am. I want to move away from pain, sorrow, and anger. I want to move toward faith, trust, and peace. Help me!" He's waiting for you to express the desire to move—He will help you; you can't do it on your own. As you surrender to your Father, He'll direct the Holy Spirit within you to comfort you and to remind you of the truth of God's character and His Word (John 14:26). Jesus' strength will help you choose to move from weak to strong, from questions to answers, from doubt to trust, and from defeat to victory.

Don't you know Satan's reaction to this? He doesn't want you to turn to God. He doesn't want you to move out of your pain and despair. Every chance he gets, Satan will flood your mind with natural, negative thoughts and emotions. I can't say it enough: *"The one who is in you is greater than the one who is in the world"* (1 John 4:4). Don't try to fight Satan alone—surrender your thoughts to the Holy Spirit and He'll rise up against Satan to bring victory with God's truth (Ephesians 6:11).

When someone asks how you're doing, your thoughts might scream, "I'm doing horrible! I'm exhausted. Let me give you a laundry list of everything that's gone wrong in the past year . . ." If you hear someone praise God's goodness in their life, your natural reaction might be, "God allowed me to suffer. I don't want to hear about the blessings in your life." Perhaps a friend calls you to join her for an afternoon out or invites your family over for the evening; you might think, as I sometimes do, "I'm so tired. I just want to go to bed. I can hide there, where I'm safe. Maybe I'll be better next week."

The real panic might come when God prompts people in your church and community to ask you to begin serving Him again. You heart pounds and your thoughts scream, "I'm incapable of getting out of bed in the morning—how am I supposed to do THAT?"

What thoughts from Satan fill your mind and hinder you from moving back into life now that the storm has passed?

_____

_____

_____

_____

How do you gain victory over the powerful, negative thoughts that capture your mind and emotions? *You* can't—but Jesus can! As soon as these paralyzing thoughts form, cry out, "Jesus, fill me with Your thoughts!" If Satan fills your mind with how hard life has been, ask the Holy Spirit to remind you of something that's made you smile lately . . . the antics of a stranger's

> *God's truths take the pity out of the party and turn it into a celebration of God's love.*

baby in the grocery store a couple of days ago? Playing with your dog? An "I love you" from someone dear to you? When Satan tempts you with the pity party prison, ask God to replace these thoughts with a statement of His truth, proclaiming who you are in Christ. You are His child! He is constantly with you and will *never* leave you or forsake you. His grace, mercy, and faithfulness *are* everlasting. These truths take the pity out of the party and turn it into a celebration of God's love. With His help, you will soon be doing a victory dance!

Is this going to be a one-time thing? I wish! It'll take time for you to choose the Holy Spirit's voice over Satan's. It isn't an easy choice to make; you'll try and fail many times, but keep at it. Satan's voice is so silky smooth as he murmurs lies to you, hoping to keep you captive. I've experienced this in my own life. For many years, I chose to believe the belittling lies I was told in my childhood. This belief was responsible for many storms I've experienced and often caused me to disobey God because I believed I was incapable of doing what He asked of me. I was in my thirties before I chose to surrender this lie to God and ask Him to show me and help me accept a true definition of who I am in Christ. It took several years of stumbles and falls before I gained the confidence to serve Him. Don't expect miracles. Hang in there and let God work in your heart and mind. Joy and victory will come in the morning (Psalm 30:5).

When I hear Satan whisper lies to me, I refute them by telling him, "Jesus has defeated you and He's commanded you to go away! God's power is infinitely greater than yours and He's holding me in His hand. You cannot touch what He's protecting. I am His child and you have no rights to me or my life." As I repeat these words, I gain confidence in God's love and protection, and His truth drowns out Satan's lies.

Ask God to help you write a statement you can repeat to counteract Satan's lies. Write it on your Faith Focus card under the title "Confidence."

_____

_____

_____

_____

Sometimes the storm moves on and time passes, but you're stuck in exhaustion, pain, or fear. When others talk about good times in their lives, you can only think about that devastating time. You don't see how you'll ever be happy or be able to trust God again. You can name the promises you believe He hasn't kept. How can He say He loves you yet allow you to experience such pain?

I've stood where you are. Even though my storm was gone, its sounds echoed in my mind. The sorrow, the fear, the paralysis became the only world I knew. Hope turned into disillusionment. Prayers were answered no, until I believed God's only intent was to hurt me. How could I ever turn to Him again? Yet, how could I live without Him? Romans 8:31 says, *"If God is for us, who can be against us?"* But I feared God had turned against me. I knew there was no other power on Earth mighty enough to stand with me! I was trapped in darkness, with no means of escape—even worse, no hope of escape.

One night, God prompted me to consider what Mary, Jesus' mother, must have felt as she watched her Son humiliated and then killed on a Roman cross. What agony did she feel in those terrible hours? Had God revealed His Son's mission in the days before she stood at the foot of the cross? If not, she must've thought every promise spoken to her during her pregnancy and during His childhood was a cruel hoax.

Yet, where do we find her as He died? She chose to move out of her anger and confusion to stand at the foot of the cross, to express her love and give her meager strength to her dying Son (John 19:25). She refused to be paralyzed by her grief. What she'd suffered was much greater than my pain, yet she stood while I cowered. Where do we find her in the long days after His burial, resurrection, and ascension—before the power of the Holy Spirit descended and when the believers gathered in fear to pray? She joined constantly together in prayer with the disciples and believers (Acts 1:14). She chose to move out of her doubt and to cling with all her heart to Jesus' promise of coming power.

In those moments God held out His hand to me and whispered that I, too, could choose to move—out of darkness into the light of hope, out of paralysis into renewed strength, out of disbelief into belief in His promises for my life. I took His hand and so can you. It will be a slow process, and it won't begin until you choose to move. Once you do, God will carry you until you're strong enough to walk on your own (Isaiah 46:4).

Our wounds won't completely heal until we choose to move from anger or disappointment toward forgiveness; from darkness toward light; from self-pity toward praise. God is holding out His hand. I challenge you to stop nursing your wounds. Do you need to move from sorrow to joy (Isaiah 51:11)? From bitterness to sweetness (Exodus 15:23–25)? From fear to peace (John 14:27)? What move do you need to make? Take your Father's hand and walk with Him away from pain to healing.

 What wounds do you have that need God's healing touch? Choose a verse that describes the restoring power you need (for example, His peace, joy, or ability to forgive). Record that verse on your Faith Focus card under the title "Healing."

_____

_____

_____

_____

When the Enemy comes to reopen old wounds, claim God's blessings and soon your wounds will be healed and you'll be strengthened beyond Satan's power to do harm. It's God's desire for you to be freed from the pain and sorrow holding you captive—freed to the joy and abundant life rightfully yours as a child of God. Choose to move from your past into your future. Surrender your chains to Him. If you don't have the strength to choose freedom, tell Him you want to make that choice. He will give you the desire of your heart. Soon you'll be celebrating freedom!

It's God's desire for you to be freed from the pain and sorrow holding you captive—freed to the joy and abundant life rightfully yours as a child of God.

CHOOSE CONTENTMENT

This is a hard one. I admit there are things in my past that still unsettle my soul. Some days I'm okay with them, other days—not so good. There are days when I go to God and ask for an explanation, demanding an answer. Usually it's when I'm already experiencing a trial; then the Enemy reminds me of this thing from the past. His goal is to throw me off balance so I can't deal with my current problems. That's why these choices are so critical. Every correct choice we make removes a weapon from the Enemy's arsenal. Someday, we will say with the apostle Paul:

> *"For I have learned to be content whatever the circumstances. I know what it is to be in need, and I know what it is to have plenty. I have learned the secret of being content in any and every situation, whether well fed or hungry, whether living in plenty or in want. I can do all things through him who gives me strength."* (Philippians 4:11–13)

What does "contentment" mean to you?

_____

_____

_____

God can surely provide the strength we need to be content in our difficult circumstances.

How did you define contentment? "Peace, happiness, quiet"? Those are words I would use. The Greek word Paul used in Philippians 4:11–13 means "to suffice or to be sufficient, to be satisfied with one's lot."[11] Notice, his word didn't mean he was at peace or that all was quiet with his soul. He didn't say he was happy. He'd allowed God to teach him to be content in any circumstance in which God placed him. He'd accepted God's provision as sufficient—even if it was meager. How'd Paul do this? What was his secret of being satisfied when things were not satisfying? What was the mystery of being able to say it was "sufficient" when he was in need? Paul told us in verse 13: *"I can do all things through him who gives me strength."* He was able to be content in an uncomfortable situation through the strength Christ gave him.

We've all heard Philippians 4:13 countless times. We often quote these words when we face a crisis. We say, "I know I can handle this because *'I can do all things through Christ wh[o] strengthen[s] me.'*" But, in Philippians 4:13, Paul isn't calling upon Christ's strength to fight, to endure, or even to survive. He's calling on Christ's strength to be content. Our prayer should be, "Father, I desire to be content in any situation You place me in. I can do this because of the strength available to me in Jesus."

Jesus left His throne in Heaven—to be homeless in a human body; He departed from the continual praise of the seraphim and cherubim—to be ridiculed by His creation; He temporarily surrendered eternal life—to taste death, knowing He would rise again. And He was content in doing so (John 10:17, 18). God can surely provide the strength we need to be content in our difficult circumstances.

Being content in God's will or in the situations He allows to occur means you have to let go of what you want, and submit to what He wants for you. It may not make sense; it may be painful. You must trust His love and draw on Jesus' strength. The Scripture verses below describe the building blocks of contentment. Read each one and find the principle needed to build a house of contentment. Write it on the stone beside the verse and explain why that principle might be valuable in achieving contentment.

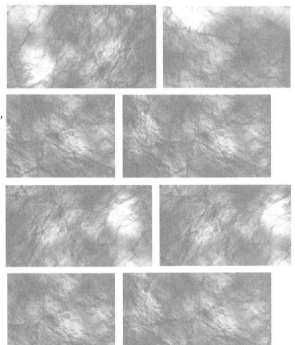

"I have been crucified with Christ and I no longer live, but Christ lives in me. The life I live in the body, I live by faith in the Son of God, who loved me." (Galatians 2:20)

"Trust in the LORD with all your heart and lean not on your own understanding." (Proverbs 3:5)

"See to it that no one takes you captive through hollow and deceptive philosophy, which depends on human tradition and the basic principles of this world rather than on Christ." (Colossians 2:8)

"Do not store up for yourselves treasures on earth . . . But store up for yourselves treasures in heaven . . . For where your treasure is, there your heart will be also." (Matthew 6:19, 20, 21)

"If you love me, you will obey what I command." (John 14:15)

Contentment is the peace that comes when we trust that God is in control of the events in our lives. When we understand that His sovereignty is steering our circumstances to complete His work in us and to prepare us for eternity, we can rest in the faithfulness of His love. To be content is not to be happy with the path we walk but to be secure in the knowledge His purposes are perfect.

Many years ago I experienced a great loss but the Lord of my life strengthened me, comforted me, and enabled me to gain the victory of contentment. Through the years, I've seen Him use this in a powerful way in my life and the lives of my loved ones. Does this mean I sing for joy because I walked through that dark valley, and watched my family endure such pain? No! But I do cherish the intimacy in my relationship with God, an intimacy I have only because of that experience. I cherish the spiritual maturity I see in my family because I know it's a result of this walk we've made together. The treasures of God's kingdom resulting from our struggles allow me to be content with my Lord's place for me.

Can you look back to a very difficult situation you now know God has used for teaching and transformation in your life? Has God given you peace and contentment in that situation? If so, how? If not, might one of the stones (verses) above help you move closer to contentment?

_____

_____

To be content is not to be happy with the path we walk but to be secure in the knowledge His purposes are perfect.

_____

_____

_____

Christ's strength is the only way you'll ever know contentment, even if you've had a life of roses! Being content with what God has given you is never easy. When storms come, and they will; when outcomes leave you stunned and questioning God's grace, and they often will—Christ's strength and kindness will gently lead you to contentment. As you read God's Word, His truth will feed your hungry heart and give you contentment. Jesus will lead you to the specific building blocks you need to construct a house of contentment. He'll enable you to reject the world's claims that you should be angry and bitter, and He'll protect you when Satan is hovering at your door. Allow contentment to settle in your soul like a beautiful fragrance.

Choose a verse that leads you to contentment wherever God has placed you. Record that verse below and on your Faith Focus card under the title "Contentment."

_____

_____

_____

It Came to Pass

When you're playing the blame-and-shame game, you can know God is not a party to it!

CHOOSE TO LEARN

As the trial fades, the "what ifs" and "if onlys" begin to haunt me. The Enemy is a master at those obsessive "ifs." He cripples us with them and causes us to place blame for everything that happened—mostly on ourselves. "If only I hadn't _____." "If only I'd said _____, surely things would've worked out differently." "It's all my fault." Those statements aren't true, and even if they were, when has placing blame ever solved anything? All we're doing is handing the Enemy a huge club and giving him permission to beat us over the head with it.

When you're playing the blame-and-shame game, you can know God is not a party to it (Psalm 34:5)! God desires for your life to be cleansed and freed of blame and shame by the blood of Jesus (Romans 8:1, 2). He desires for you and me to look at His work during the turmoil and to learn lessons that deepen our faith and lead us to a closer walk with Him.

As you look at a past crisis or a present suffering, in what way are you blaming yourself? Jesus calls you to hand it over to Him and to allow Him to set you free.

_____

_____

_____

As the storm moves off into the distance, your Father wants desperately to ease your pain. He can use the circumstances of the storm and the people around you to teach you spiritual truths that will enrich your life and deepen your relationship with Him. Is this your desire? Learning the lessons of life and of Him is your choice. How He loves to teach you, to see you grow in the image of His Son—and then to watch you reach out and touch the lives of others around you (2 Corinthians 1:4)!

It seems impossible to learn life lessons or spiritual lessons when you're exhausted. Your nerves are tighter than a circus high wire and your emotions are riding some crazy roller coaster. How are you supposed to look at the situation and learn anything? The answer's the same as always: You can't, but God can. He says to you, *"My power is made perfect in weakness,"* (2 Corinthians 12:9). When you are exhausted, He is power and strength. He gives you rest: *"He will make you lie down in green pastures, he will lead you beside quiet waters, he will restore your soul"* (Psalm 23:2, 3, author's paraphrase). When your nerves are frazzled, He calms you: *"Cast all your anxiety on him because he cares for you"* (1 Peter 5:7). Surrender your wild emotions to Him and He will comfort you: *"I will turn their mourning into gladness; I will give them comfort and joy instead of sorrow"* (Jeremiah 31:13b).

The lessons God teaches are different for each of us. Learning these lessons is your choice. If you refuse to learn them now, He'll take you through another experience to teach you what you didn't learn this time. He knows how critical these lessons are for your eternity living.

Look for a Pattern
As I look at the storms in my life, I see a pattern. Many of my trials came because I kept repeating the same destructive behavior. Surely you've heard the old adage: If you keep doing what you've always done, you'll keep getting what you've always got. I don't know about you, but I've certainly beaten my head against a few brick walls. Praise God, He is patient! There are many examples, but the one that causes the most suffering is a hurtful relationship. Do you move from one destructive friendship to another, always letting someone take advantage of you? Is this often true when it comes to the men you choose? Perhaps you allow a relationship to control you, to lead you into places and activities displeasing to your Father. Jesus moved only within His Father's will (John 5:19); allow Him to guide you. Don't allow your relationships to come at the price of your morality or integrity. Your purity as His blessed daughter is more important than any relationship.

Are many of your trials financial? Do you place your security in a bank account rather than in your Lord? Certainly God commands us to be good stewards of all He gives us, and He expects us to prepare for the future. I am sure He wants us to enjoy the possessions He's given us but to put these things at the center of our lives is to sin against Him (Luke 12:15–21). Early in our marriage, many of our crises revolved around financial problems until we recognized we didn't have a correct perspective on our money. God taught us to trust Him with all we have—and He has never let us down.

 As you consider your trials or times of suffering, do they often seem to involve the same type of struggle or a repeated behavior pattern? If so, what lesson might God be trying to teach you?

A Crisis of Faith

It is so easy to claim God as Provider, until a financial crisis rears its ugly head. We believe in Him as Healer, until someone we love is afflicted with a serious illness. He is Lord Almighty until the storm rages and we lose all sense of stability. Satan knows the point at which we are most apt to lose our trust in God and he attacks us at that very point. Our Father allows the attack—why? To teach us He is faithful in the very area in which we doubt Him most.

When the storm disappears over the horizon, we're drained. If we keep our eyes on the fading storm, we'll be walking backwards. That's just what Satan wants. We mourn the past and fear what we can't see coming. Worry swirls around our feet and causes us to stumble. Worry shouts, "God can't handle the future!"

Satan feeds on our worry. He manipulates it and tends to it until it grows into a full-blown crisis of faith. Soon, we can't sleep well and we can't eat. Worry begins to consume us. And what do we accomplish by all this? Has the wringing of hands and pacing ever gained us an extra twenty-four hours (Luke 12:25)? Has the moaning and groaning ever caused the object of our worry to disappear into thin air? I'll tell you one thing it does accomplish— it gives Satan control of our thoughts. Does that sound dangerous to you? I hope so!

What is the solution to worry and anxiety? You guessed it: God's Word. "God can't handle my problem" will be wiped out by words from Scripture that proclaim His power over your circumstances. Have you suffered health problems? Don't allow anxiety to take hold. Go to your Father, for He has the power to sustain you and guide you as you struggle to regain your health.

Are you crawling out of a financial disaster? Don't be tempted to build your security on the money in your bank account. Your Father knows your needs and He will see they are met (Matthew 6:25–34). When consequences leave your world unstable, do not doubt His power and presence. Run to Him and allow Him to shelter you, for He alone is our Safe Tower (Proverbs 18:10, 11). These words and so many others you may find will fight back the worry and will defeat Satan's attempt to gain control of your thoughts. He cannot stand in the face of truth!

Is there a point at which your faith frequently stumbles? Do you believe God can handle that? Find a Bible verse that speaks to that specific issue.

_____

_____

_____

A Crisis of Control

Sometimes trials serve to make us aware we've accepted Jesus as our Savior but not as our Lord. I like to make my own decisions. When I hear thunder rolling in the distance, I panic. If God allowed pain in the past, will He protect me in the future? Can I trust His presence when I'm still blaming Him for deserting me in the past?

> **When consequences leave your world unstable, do not doubt God's power and presence.**

Jesus is my Lord only when I turn over to Him complete control of each action and decision. This is easy on the good days, but to give God control of our actions and decisions in tough times isn't part of our nature. When storms subside, I sincerely pray, "Lord, I'll trust You next time." Then, at the smallest cloud, I leap right in and handle it my own way, as I've done so many times before.

What happened to our confessions of faith? We meant it at the time but we can't always carry through. Surrender is not something we do when we look in the mirror in the morning, but then go about our day as if we are in control. It takes being honest with Him in our weakness and then inviting Him to spend the day with us, bringing His strength into our hearts to match our weaknesses. Where we are emotionally weak, He will bring the power of His peace. When our self-control is weak, He will bring His strength and His power of self-restraint and no one will be prouder than He when we are free of that behavior.

Praise God, His mercy and grace travel with us every moment, every step! Whisper a prayer, asking Him to control your words as you walk up to that person with whom you so desperately long to restore peace. He will answer your prayer. When temptation confronts you, cry out to Him for help. He will provide you a way to escape from the temptation. As you submit to Him minute by minute, increasingly your confession and your behavior will match. The victory will come!

Is there an area in your life where storms frequently arise because you refuse to release control to God?

_____

_____

_____

_____

Your Father desires to speak to you, to teach you and to mold you through the storms in your life. You may hear God say to you as He said to Israel, *"Therefore I am going to allure her; I will lead her into the desert and speak tenderly to her"* (Hosea 2:14). No one really wants to be in the desert, but sometimes it's necessary so you'll take your eyes off the world around you—the crazy schedule you're keeping, the ladder of success you're climbing at work, the social merry-go-round you're riding—whatever it is that's put your relationship with God on the back burner. Perhaps, in this desert, God can get your attention and speak tenderly to you, "I love you. I miss your fellowship." Focus your eyes on His face. If you surrender your will to His, He'll speak to you from the storm. Please know that God would not have allowed you to experience this suffering if you could've learned these lessons any other way (1 Peter 1:6, 7).

APPLY Find a verse that describes how God speaks to and teaches you during difficult times and write it below and on your Faith Focus card under the title "Learn."

_____

_____

_____

> ## Praise God, His mercy and grace travel with us every moment, every step!

SEEK GOD'S PERSPECTIVE

Although my small brain questions this next statement, it's a fact: God has a plan, a purpose, and a perspective for every trial that enters our lives. He doesn't make things up as He goes along. He doesn't hurriedly switch from plan A to plan B as if something caught Him by surprise. Remember Jonah? The whale wasn't plan B. God's awesome plan was to save Jonah from sure death by scooping him into the belly of a whale. Sorry, but I would've vetoed that idea.

First thing, can you imagine the *smell*? Ladies, there aren't enough scented candles in the world to cover up that smell. And the weird sounds—does a whale's stomach growl? On top of that, it had to be pitch-black dark in there; not much light can come in those little blowholes—even less at night. To make matters worse, whales love to leap high up in the air and go crashing back down into the sea. Can you imagine being banged around in there for three days as the whale made its way to the beach? A smelly, dark roller coaster that makes you seasick doesn't sound like deliverance to me. How about you? Well, it sounded like deliverance to Jonah. Listen to his words, spoken from inside the whale: *"But you brought my life up from the pit, O LORD my God"* (Jonah 2:6b).

Jonah 2 recorded the first words he prayed, but I have to believe there were some panicky ones spoken before these official church-type words. Maybe they went something like this: "Oy vey! Now I've been eaten by a whale! I could've drowned and been dead already. But, no, I have to sit here in the smelly dark." But, through God's strength, Jonah was able to see his situation from God's perspective, and the complaints we might expect became a prayer of praise and thanksgiving (Jonah 2:1–9).

Perspective. The dictionary defines it as a point of view: "the ability to view things in their true relationship." Let's adapt that definition a little: the ability to view our times of suffering in their true relationship to God's plans and purposes.

When we look back at our storms, we often do so through the lens of anger and pain. How can anything good could ever come out of such agony? We might turn to society's coping skills: Pretend it didn't happen, drown in self-pity, or dream of vengeance. What a difference it makes when we look at our past through the lens of God's truth! When we trust His love, what we gain becomes more powerful than what we might lose. How much deeper is your faith? How much richer is your relationship with your Father? Allow Him to reveal the blessings He's formed out of the departing clouds. With God's perspective, your "whale" becomes a blessing in disguise.

APPLY What difficult event in your life became a blessing when seen with God's perspective?

_____

_____

_____

_____

What a difference it makes when we look at our past through the lens of God's truth!

Only when we trust God can we see our trials through His eyes. Our own thoughts will lead us astray; God's truth will reveal His plans and purposes. The world's approach will leave us trapped in the past; God's guidance will show us His perspective and reveal His blessings.

God's Faithful Promise

> *"For I know the plans I have for you," declares the* LORD, *"plans to prosper you and not to harm you, plans to give you hope and a future."* (Jeremiah 29:11)

What a wonderful promise—and yet, in the shadow of a retreating storm, it's easy to believe that God hasn't kept His word. When our lives are in shambles, the harm is very real. Do we measure the truth of God's faithfulness against our circumstances and find Him lacking? Let's examine the truth of this verse.

"For I know the plans I have for you," declares the LORD, . . .
The Hebrew word used here for "plans" means "purpose or intention."[12] God is sovereign. We are not cosmic accidents; our lives have meaning and purpose. God plans each day intentionally to bring about His purpose.

> *"All the days ordained for me were written in your book before one of them came to be."* (Psalm 139:16b)

> *"Many are the plans in a man's heart, but it is the* LORD's *purpose that prevails."* (Proverbs 19:21)

> *"For we are God's workmanship, created in Christ Jesus to do good works, which God prepared in advance for us to do."* (Ephesians 2:10)

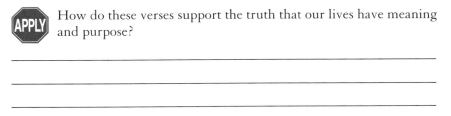 How do these verses support the truth that our lives have meaning and purpose?

_____

_____

_____

_____

". . . plans to prosper you and not to harm you, . . ."
This phrase gets me every time. Here's my initial interpretation of these words: "Plans to make me prosperous (i.e., having everything I need and a few things I want) and to never let me be seriously or unfairly hurt." Of course, I don't expect a fairy-tale existence. I just want what I think this promises. But do we really understand what this promises?

The Hebrew word translated "prosper" means "peace and completeness."[13] But what about wealth and worldly comforts? God isn't concerned with our worldly comfort. He's focused on re-creating us in the image of His Son. Even when we're in distress, He gives us peace, and promises to complete the transforming work He's begun in us.

> *"Peace I leave with you; my peace I give you. I do not give to you as the world gives. Do not let your hearts be troubled and do not be afraid."* (John 14:27)

God plans each day intentionally to bring about His purpose.

"Being confident of this, that he who began a good work in you will carry it on to completion until the day of Christ Jesus." (Philippians 1:6)

"And the peace of God, which transcends all understanding, will guard your hearts and your minds in Christ Jesus." (Philippians 4:7)

How do the verses above promise God's peace and completion, no matter our circumstances?

_____

_____

_____

_____

He gives us peace and He keeps us from harm. The Hebrew word used for "harm" in Jeremiah 29:11 means "evil"—not just your garden-variety evil, but *absolute* evil.[14] It doesn't refer to the storms we face in life, even the serious ones. If He allows suffering, what's He keeping us from? Let's look to 1 John 5:18 for the answer: *"The one [Jesus] who was born of God keeps him [God's child] safe, and the evil one cannot harm him."*

As God's children, we are in a fight against the powers of this dark world and against the spiritual forces of evil (Ephesians 6:12). As long as we live on this earth, Satan is on the attack. He wants us to focus on our trials and to doubt God's love, provision, and power. But all his efforts are in vain. For now and eternity, you belong to God and He will keep you from the Evil One. Satan can't harm our lives or our souls, because we are held in the hand of God.

> **Satan can't harm our lives or our souls, because we are held in the hand of God.**

"He guards the lives of his faithful ones and delivers them from the hand of the wicked." (Psalm 97:10b)

"But the Lord is faithful, and he will strengthen and protect you from the evil one." (2 Thessalonians 3:3)

"My prayer is not that you take them out of the world but that you protect them from the evil one." (John 17:15)

How do the verses above promise God's protection?

_____

_____

_____

_____

". . . plans to give you hope and a future."

Oh, how our small minds miss the greatness God envisions for us! The "here and now" is all we know. Of course God cares about our lives now, but He recognizes that this time is but a blip on the scale in comparison with the eternity we'll have with Him. His perspective is based on the whole of our lives: the "here and now" and the "there and forever"! This is but our preschool training yard. It's a shadow of our real life. We are aliens, travelers on a journey on the way to our final destination: Our true home is with

Jesus and our Father (2 Corinthians 5:1). Jeremiah 29:11 says, *"Plans to give you hope* (the Hebrew word meaning hope, expectation, attitude of anticipation with the expectation that something will happen[15]) *and a future"* (the Hebrew word meaning the end, last time, or latter time[16]). He's not dwelling on the "future" we have here. He's trying to pull our gaze beyond this earth, full of trouble on a good day, to Heaven, where we'll rejoice and serve Him forever.

> *"Come, you who are blessed by my Father; take your inheritance, the kingdom prepared for you since the creation of the world."* (Matthew 25:34)

> *"I am going there to prepare a place for you. And if I go and prepare a place for you, I will come back and take you to be with me that you also may be where I am."* (John 14:2b, 3)

> *"No eye has seen, no ear has heard, no mind has conceived what God has prepared for those who love him."* (1 Corinthians 2:9)

APPLY How do these verses encourage you to keep your eyes on the "there and forever?"

_____

_____

_____

_____

How should we look at the message of Jeremiah 29:11? Might I suggest a paraphrase? Let me stress that this is *my* interpretation of this beautiful verse, given the Hebrew meanings we've examined. *"For I know the purposes I have for you," declares the LORD, "purposes for peace and completeness, and not for absolute evil, to give you an anticipation and expectation for your end time."* This has a different flavor, doesn't it? God's protection in this life and our glorious, eternal inheritance are beyond doubt. I know that I know I will spend eternity with my Jesus. The thought of seeing His face, the face of the One who was willing to die for me in order to give me life—that thought fills me with such excitement, this life seems trivial! Perhaps that's the perspective with which He desires us to see as we read Jeremiah 29:11.

We've been through many verses as we've sought God's perspective on our struggles and suffering. Has one touched your heart? Write it below and on your Faith Focus card under the title "Understanding."

_____

_____

_____

_____

Have you ever wondered how Jesus kept putting one foot in front of the other when He knew the cross was waiting for Him? By keeping His eyes set beyond the cross toward His true destination:

> *"Let us fix our eyes on Jesus . . . who for the joy set before him endured the cross, scorning its shame, and sat down at the right hand of the throne of God."* (Hebrews 12:2, emphasis added)

God's protection in this life and our glorious, eternal inheritance are beyond doubt.

As you look back on the storms in your life, remember that this life lasts but a brief time and we'll be with Him forever! I don't know what we'll be doing for eternity but I'm sure it'll be beyond anything we can imagine. For now, God will take you *"from strength to strength"* (Psalm 84:7a), enabling you to meet the challenges before you. Jesus will be beside you, guiding you and upholding you until each choice is made and He brings you to victory: a new life of rejoicing, filled with shouts of joy (Psalm 105:43). Then, one day, for the joy set before *you*, you will reach the new Jerusalem, with streets of gold, the river of life, and the glory of the Lord as its light. Look beyond life's storms; watch for the sparkle of gold and your Father's smile—just over the horizon.

8

The Journey

As I have walked through this study with you, God has taught me many truths. He's reminded me that without Him, I can do nothing. He's shown me I must walk with Him and make some hard choices if I truly want to become a woman of faith.

Have you been blessed by the lives of the men and women in Scripture whom we've studied? I certainly see a reflection of myself in each one. Sometimes I'm frightened, often I'm angry. I'm hounded by doubts and I grasp for any way out of my sorrow rather than follow God through it.

As wonderful as these accounts have been, they're meaningless if the truths are not applied to our individual situations. God's Word loses its power if we leave it lying on the pages instead of allowing it to rise up in our lives.

Through the lives of the men and women in Scripture, we learned how the power of God accomplishes amazing things in our hearts and our lives as He prepares us for eternity living. Nowhere is this truer than in the account of Martha, Mary, and Lazarus told in John 11. Jesus deliberately allowed a storm to rage in their lives so He could do *"more than all we ask or imagine, according to his power"* (Ephesians 3:20).

DARK CLOUDS GATHER: A MESSAGE OF FAITH

The account of one of the most staggering miracles Jesus performed during His ministry is found in John 11. In this chapter, Jesus demonstrated the reality of His victory over death and His promise of eternal life. But we mustn't forget that this event involved real people with real fears and emotions. Mary and Martha loved their brother, Lazarus, and were devastated at his death—a death they knew Jesus could've prevented. Although most of what follows wasn't detailed in Scripture, we can learn so much from viewing the story through Mary and Martha's eyes. Let's allow them to be human and to express all the emotions we might've had in the same situation.

As the scene opens, Jesus and His disciples are across the Jordan. Mary, her sister Martha, and their brother, Lazarus, are at home in Bethany, a village just outside Jerusalem.

> *"Now a man named Lazarus was sick. He was from Bethany, the village of Mary and her sister Martha . . . whose brother Lazarus now lay sick."* (John 11:1, 2).

Lazarus became sick—perhaps something was going around. He was a man, so he wouldn't have paid much attention to it at first. Ladies, what is it about men? My husband's the same way. He's susceptible to sinus infections. When I begin to notice the early symptoms, I usually ask if he's getting sick. He insists it's just allergies until he's too sick to deny it any longer. I imagine Lazarus reacting to his sisters the same way: No, he didn't need to stay home from work. No, he didn't need them fussing over him. He was just fine, thank you very much!

At some point, even Lazarus had to admit he wasn't feeling well. Perhaps He stayed home. He lay around sick while Mary and Martha tried all the home remedies they knew. I suspect friends dropped in to offer their favorite family remedies, some of which probably tasted terrible! If there was a village prayer chain, Lazarus's name was on it.

When Lazarus continued to get worse, I'm sure his two sisters worried even more. Perhaps they called in someone famous in the field of medicine arts. What began as a common illness became serious. Do you think the two sisters sensed dark clouds gathering? How do you think they felt, watching Lazarus grow more ill while they exhausted every solution they knew? Were Mary and Martha desperate for help as Lazarus got worse?

How do you think Mary and Martha prayed during this time?

_____

_____

_____

_____

I'm sure their prayers were honest and heartfelt and they believed that God could heal Lazarus. Jesus visited with them right before Lazarus became ill. Did they think, "If only Jesus had stayed with us a little longer, then He would've been here when we needed Him." Did they feel abandoned by their friend, their Lord? We've all felt that way when things started going downhill. We've all felt that God wasn't around when we needed Him.

What should Mary and Martha do? Should they wait to see if their prayers were answered? Should they wait for Jesus to return? Should they send for Him? Imagine their conversation:

Martha: Should we send for Jesus?

Mary: He's Lord and Messiah . . . He probably already knows and He's on His way.

Martha: But what if He doesn't know?

Mary: Don't get so anxious, Martha. We've prayed as Jesus taught us, right?

Martha: Well, Lazarus has been sick for so long. And we've tried every remedy we know. I'd just feel better if Jesus was here.

Mary: But He's a day's journey away. By the time our message gets to Him and He travels back, two days will have passed. Lazarus will probably be up and around by then and we will have taken Jesus away from His teaching for nothing.

Martha: For nothing? Have you looked at Lazarus this morning? He's not getting better, he's getting worse. Two days will be too long. We could lose him by then. Jesus loves Lazarus; He needs to know!

Mary: All right, send Eli. He's been to the Jordan with Jesus before and he'll find Him quickly.

If you had been in their place, what would your message to Jesus have said?

_____

_____

_____

"So the sisters sent word to Jesus, 'Lord, the one you love is sick.'" (John 11:3)

The words of this message reveal a lot about Mary and Martha and their faith in Jesus. What's *not* said in this message is just as important as what was said. The sisters didn't panic and tell Jesus that Lazarus was dying. They didn't beg Jesus to come quickly. Now let's look closer at what they did say.

"Lord . . ." What a beautiful acknowledgement of His lordship in their lives! He was their friend and, above all, He was their *Lord*. This word speaks of love, trust, and surrender. It's easy to allow Jesus to be our Savior and not our Lord. It's easy to trust Him when life's good, but when storm clouds build in the distance it's hard to surrender to His lordship. When the future

When the future is unknown, surrender takes real faith, not lip-service faith.

"For I am convinced that neither death nor life, neither angels nor demons, neither the present nor the future, nor any powers, neither height nor depth, nor anything else in all creation, will be able to separate us from the love of God that is in Christ Jesus our Lord."

Romans 8:38-39

is unknown, surrender takes real faith, not lip-service faith. Even so, to bow before Him and whisper, "Jesus is Lord," brings peace, strength, and the assurance of His presence and sovereignty.

". . . the one you love . . ." No mention is made of Lazarus's name. Do you hear the quiet confidence in those four words—*"the one you love"*? When you look out the window and see dark clouds gathering, can you say, "Lord, it's me, the one you love!"? If you don't feel that assurance, talk to someone you trust who can help you find it within the pages of God's Word.

Because of my difficult relationship with my earthly father, I struggled to believe in the unconditional love of my heavenly Father. A sweet friend encouraged me to rewrite John 17:6–26 as though Jesus prayed just for me. I placed my name (or "she" or "her") in the verses as I rewrote them to refer to one person. When I read the prayer through, I was so moved by Jesus' love that I no longer feared His rejection. He is the One who loves me. He is the One who loves you.

> *"I have summoned you by name; you are mine."* (Isaiah 43:1b)

> *"I have loved you with an everlasting love; I have drawn you with loving-kindness."* (Jeremiah 31:3)

> *"How great is the love the Father has lavished on us, that we should be called the children of God!"* (1 John 3:1)

> *"This is how we know what love is: Jesus Christ laid down his life for us."* (1 John 3:16)

How do these verses confirm God's deep love for you?

_____

_____

_____

_____

Nothing can separate us from our Father's love (Romans 8:38, 39)! It is beyond our understanding.

". . . is sick . . ." The message ends with a simple declaration of the circumstances. Boy, is this ever different from my prayers! I tell Him the situation, give detailed instructions on what I want done, and conclude with the desired results. If everything's not done by the next day, I chide Him gently and repeat all the details, in case He's forgotten. Am I wrong to do that? It's never wrong to tell our Father what we want! Jesus teaches us that in the parable of the persistent widow (Luke 18:1–8). But it is wrong to give Him orders and expect Him to obey us!

Mary and Martha showed pure trust in the sovereignty of God by their simple words. They presented the situation to Jesus and left it in His hands. They believed He could cure Lazarus by a word spoken across the miles, as He did the centurion's servant (Luke 7:1–10). If He decided to come, they believed God could keep Lazarus alive until Jesus' arrival. They chose to trust His decision.

How hard is this to do? How hard is it to come to your Lord, lay your problem at His feet, and then walk away? Do you trust Him to deal with the looming storm?

APPLY As you've journeyed through this study, what have you learned that allows you to place an uncertain future in His hands?

_____

_____

_____

_____

_____

_____

_____

_____

_____

Bethany is about twenty miles from the Jordan River, and Jesus was a short distance across the river (John 10:40). To travel these twenty to thirty miles would've taken a whole day. The messenger Mary and Martha sent reached Jesus the next day. When Jesus heard Lazarus was ill, He decided to wait two more days (John 11:6). The morning of the fourth day, Jesus decided it was time to make the long trip to Bethany. When He arrived, He discovered Lazarus had been dead and in the tomb for four days (John 11:17).

Lazarus was dead. The storm no longer hovered on the horizon; it had struck with full force. As the days passed, Mary and Martha heard nothing from Jesus. It was over; hope was gone. But, dear one, hope is never gone when Jesus is with us!

THE STORM STRIKES: PREPARED BY SUFFERING

The Journey

DAY TWO

Hurrying from Bethany, the messenger arrived in the area and searched until he found Jesus. He told Jesus of Lazarus's illness; Jesus gave him a message to take back to Mary and Martha:

"When he heard this, Jesus said, 'This sickness will not end in death. No, it is for God's glory so that God's Son may be glorified through it.' Jesus loved Martha and her sister and Lazarus. Yet when he heard that Lazarus was sick, he stayed where he was two more days." (John 11:4–6)

These words from Jesus might seem a little coldhearted. My humble opinion is that not every word uttered by Jesus is recorded in Scripture. Surely Jesus asked the messenger questions about His dear friends! I imagine He

It's hard to trust God when His actions are the opposite of your prayer requests.

asked how Lazarus's symptoms had progressed, what treatments they'd tried, and how Mary and Martha were doing, just as you and I would.

The poor messenger was probably prancing around, eager for Jesus to return to Bethany, but he could tell by these strange words Jesus wasn't going anywhere soon. The *"not end in death"* part sounded great, but what did the *"God's glory"* and *"Son may be glorified"* stuff mean? Jesus could fix the whole thing right now by just going back with him! It all made sense to the messenger, but there he stood with a message from Jesus that he couldn't quite understand and a clear signal that Jesus wasn't returning with him. Jesus' actions were the opposite of what Mary and Martha wanted and needed. Often, when a storm strikes, it's hard to find comfort in God's Word. It's hard to trust Him when His actions are the opposite of your prayer requests.

What have the past six weeks taught you about God that might help you respond in this situation?

_____

_____

_____

_____

_____

_____

_____

_____

_____

Jesus didn't budge and the messenger headed home, probably afraid he'd be in big trouble when he got there because Jesus wasn't with him. As he approached the house, he could see signs of mourning. Ladies, do you think he tried to sneak in without being noticed? Or do you think his grief overcame him as he ran in to verify what he already knew?

When Mary and Martha saw him, what do you think they did? Did they immediately look around for Jesus? Can you imagine them searching the crowded room of mourners for His face—the tender, loving face they needed so much? After a few minutes they must've realized Jesus wasn't there. Did they begin to overwhelm the poor messenger with questions?

Mary: Did you find Jesus?

Messenger: Yes, I found Him and talked to Him.

Martha: Didn't He understand about Lazarus, and that we needed Him?

Messenger: Yes, He asked me to describe my master's illness and He seemed very upset. He asked tenderly about both of my mistresses.

Mary: Why didn't He come? What did He say? We need Him.

(The messenger hesitates, starts to answer, then doesn't.)

Mary: What did He say? Did He say when He's coming? Certainly He sent a message!

Messenger: Yes, He sent a message. He said, *"This sickness will not end in death. It is for God's glory so that His Son will be glorified through it."*

Can you imagine the stunned silence? What thoughts went through the two grieving sisters' minds? *"This sickness will not end in death."*?! But Lazarus was already dead! Had Jesus lost touch with reality over there? *God's glory?* . . . *His* glory? How can Lazarus's death bring God glory? Jesus' words made no sense; His actions made no sense. None of this made any sense!

The storm—the painful loss of their beloved brother—hit them full force. It hit in spite of their desperate prayers. It hit in spite of their pleas to Jesus. I've been there; you have, too. You prayed but the words seemed to hang in the air, unanswered. You read promises in Scripture but the words sat on the page and brought you no comfort. The storm hit, taking your breath away. Like Mary and Martha, you searched for some hint of God's love and power in the madness of the storm but you felt lost and abandoned.

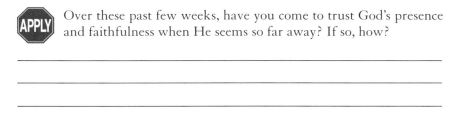 Over these past few weeks, have you come to trust God's presence and faithfulness when He seems so far away? If so, how?

_____

_____

_____

_____

Of course, Jesus had told them about the promise of everlasting life for the believer. They knew that those who believed in Him would never really die (John 11:23, 24). Could this be what He meant by *"This sickness will not end in death"*? The promise of seeing their brother again at the resurrection was a beautiful truth, but the pain of loss was *now*.

Can you identify with these thoughts? I can. Over the years, when a believing friend or family member lost a loved one, I'd offer comfort with the promise they'd be together again. I'd try to comfort them by telling them their loved one was with the Lord, having a whiz-bang welcome party!

When my Mom died, I knew she immediately moved into the purplest mansion you ever saw and entered into a gabfest that would go on for several eternities. Her joy was and is unimaginable! I knew beyond any doubt I'd see her again. But you know what? Those facts didn't give me near as much comfort as I thought they would. She wasn't with me, and during those first months, that's what mattered. My grief obscured my view of eternity.

The storm engulfed Mary and Martha. One moment they were trying another treatment, recommended by a neighbor, on Lazarus—and the next, Lazarus was gone. All this with no sign of Jesus. Our storms often come upon us without warning as well. We search desperately for God's hand in our circumstances and we can't find Him. Is He here? Is He coming? Is He going to let us down? We read His Word and it doesn't make any sense. People around us try to encourage us with His words—words we've heard all our lives—but they sound like a foreign language. They sound completely out of touch with the reality we are facing.

When the storm is raging through your life, what cords do you have that tether you to your foundation of faith? How might your Faith Focus card help you?

_____

_____

_____

_____

_____

_____

_____

God often chooses to apply His great power to our hearts rather than to our circumstances.

God is bigger than your reality! He's bigger than my reality. He is so much bigger than the ever-so-small understanding we have of Him. Do you believe God is more powerful than your situation? Do you believe He's bigger than the suffering you face today or the unresolved pain you carry from the past? Dear one, He is! Understand that, in His sovereignty, He will choose how to bring His greatness into your circumstance, either to deliver you or to carry you through.

> *"Yours, O LORD, is the greatness and the power and the glory and the majesty and the splendor, for everything in heaven and earth is yours."* (1 Chronicles 29:11)

> *"You are the God who performs miracles; you display your power among the peoples."* (Psalm 77:14)

> *"And his [God's] incomparably great power for us who believe. That power is like the working of his mighty strength, which he exerted in Christ when he raised him from the dead."* (Ephesians 1:19, 20a)

APPLY How do the Scriptures above proclaim God's greatness?

_____

_____

_____

_____

_____

_____

_____

Infinite power. Unimaginable power. All at our fingertips. But God often chooses to apply His great power to our hearts rather than to our circumstances. His power heals doubts. His power overcomes fear. God is more powerful than any situation we face. It is His power that carries us through.

Is there a specific situation in your life you're afraid is beyond God's power to overcome? Do you think your sorrow, doubt, or fear are beyond God's power to heal? If so, stand on the truth of the verses cited above and use the blanks below to declare your faith in the greatness of God's power in your situation.

I, _____, proclaim that God is greater than

_____.

Mary and Martha believed in Jesus' power. They believed His power could heal any illness and conquer death. But He didn't come when they needed Him. Did they begin to question their faith in Him? Did they begin to doubt His love—how could He love them if He allowed Lazarus to die?

Was Jesus powerless to comfort Mary and Martha or to heal Lazarus? No! He was fully God and had proved His power many times. Was His love for His friends only an act? No! He loved them deeply, richly, with a love beyond human understanding.

Why, then, did Jesus tarry on the other side of the Jordan instead of returning to Bethany? He could have healed Lazarus from across the Jordan. He could've willed Lazarus to live until He reached Bethany and then healed him. As wonderful as either of these healings would've been, it would not have stretched the two sisters' faith. It wouldn't have brought them face-to-face with a new knowledge of God. God used their suffering to prepare their hearts and minds to accept the most miraculous event they would ever see.

Mary and Martha defined reality by their circumstances and emotions. Isn't that how we are? When things go well, I feel good; therefore, God is good. When things are hard, my emotions are in turmoil; therefore, God is unfair and hurtful. My reality is based on what I experienced yesterday, what's going on right now, and what I expect to happen tomorrow.

God's reality is based on His knowledge of my life today, next month, ten years from now, and into eternity. He sees my entire life; I can't see past the end of my nose. He knows when I'll have good times, valley times, waiting times; He knows how all the pieces fit together to make a beautiful life that glorifies Him. I just want the good times to roll.

That's the nature of a storm, isn't it? A shift in reality. A warp in the world. An abnormality in your normalcy. In your present reality, in your measured world, perhaps a bigger view of God won't fit. If you're like me, He's snuggled in there just nicely as He is. I don't want any stretching, any challenging, or any non-comfort-zone living. All of that hurts. Let me repeat that. Trials hurt. Suffering hurts. They force us to ask questions we'd never ask at any other time. To hear answers we'd never hear otherwise. To encounter a fullness in God we could never know apart from the experience. Through it all we learn this: When everything else is gone, God is there.

Through suffering, we encounter a fullness in God we could never know apart from the experience.

TAKING STEPS . . . TOWARD JESUS

How my heart hurts for Mary and Martha as I think about them grieving the loss of their brother. I have a beloved sister. I can't imagine life without her. My grief would be unbearable if I lost her. Her love and friendship mean more to me than words can express.

How my heart hurts for my Jesus! He's the One who held children in His arms to bless them. He's the One whose heart was tender toward outcasts: lepers, women who were bleeding, Samaritans. He's the One who, at the end of the day—when He must've been exhausted—couldn't turn away the multitudes who came to Him to be healed (Matthew 8:14–16; Mark 1:40–42; John 4). But now He must wait to go heal His dear friend Lazarus. He couldn't go comfort Mary and Martha. Even though He knew the reasons He must wait, can you imagine how His heart must've been breaking? How hard was it for Him to resist snapping His fingers and saying, "Lazarus, be healed!"?

APPLY Have you considered how God might grieve when you walk through times of hardship or crisis? Have the past few weeks changed your view of His heart toward you as you experience trials? If so, how?

_____

_____

_____

_____

_____

_____

Even now, our Father grieves when we suffer!

Even as the Father whispered to His Son in the Garden of Gethsemane, "There is no other way but the cross," sometimes He must whisper to us there's no way other than the path leading through the valley of suffering. Our suffering never brings Him pleasure. The book of Judges describes a series of times God brought discipline on the nation of Israel because the people repeatedly turned away from worshipping Him as the one true God. Judges 10:16 describes how He felt during these times of punishment and I believe it describes how He feels when we're experiencing suffering: *"His soul was grieved for the misery of Israel"* (KJV). I'm sure Jesus grieved for the misery Mary and Martha were experiencing, even though He knew their sorrow would soon turn to joy (Jeremiah 31:13). Even now, our Father grieves when we suffer!

After waiting two days, Jesus left the far side of the Jordan and traveled to Bethany. Imagine the murmurs racing through Bethany as Jesus approached the outskirts of town. Everyone knew of His friendship with Mary and Martha. Perhaps some wondered, What good did that friendship do them when Lazarus's life was at stake? I'm sure it wasn't long before news of Jesus' approach reached Mary and Martha. How did they feel when they heard He was coming? What would you have felt? My thoughts betray me. When I put myself in their place, hurtful words such as "Why bother to come now? You didn't come when we needed you and we don't want to see you now" rumble around in my mind.

In spite of what she may have felt, Martha went to meet Jesus. He was her Savior, where else could she go? Many times I've wanted to turn away from God but He's all I have! There is no life without Him. I can't imagine the pain in her heart as she padded down the path toward Him. What did she feel when her eyes first met His? I believe she responded to the sorrow and love she saw in His face, and knew beyond any doubt that her Lord loved her.

How has God shown His love for you even though you came to Him with a heart full of questions?

_____

_____

_____

_____

Let's listen in on Martha and Jesus as they meet:

> *"'Lord,' Martha said to Jesus, 'if you had been here, my brother would not have died. But I know that even now God will give you whatever you ask.'*
>
> *Jesus said to her, 'Your brother will rise again.'*
>
> *Martha answered, 'I know he will rise again in the resurrection at the last day.'*
>
> *Jesus said to her, 'I am the resurrection and the life. He who believes in me will live, even though he dies; and whoever lives and believes in me will never die. Do you believe this?'*
>
> *'Yes, Lord,' she told him, 'I believe that you are the Christ, the Son of God, who was to come into the world.'"* (John 11:21–27)

"If . . ." Martha stood before Jesus, looked Him in the eyes and expressed her grief, her desire for things to have been different. *"If you had been here . . ."* Martha was able to speak openly and honestly to her Lord, standing face-to-face with Him. There've been times when I've cried out from the midst of a storm, "IF You'd been here . . . ; IF You had willed differently . . . then this would not have happened." Have you ever cried out "IF" to God? Like Martha, we've all been hurt when God's will didn't match ours. In our plan, no one would've suffered and no one would've died. Everyone would've lived happily ever after. God's will brought pain; God's will allowed Lazarus to die. IF God had listened to us, then all this would've been avoided.

Listen to Martha's words. She didn't remain in the *"If . . ."* of the past. She allowed her faith to move her on to the "now." She might have seen Jesus' power heal before; she'd certainly heard the disciples describe how He'd raised the dead. Jesus was still her Lord; He was still God's Son. She believed He had His Father's ear and had access to His Father's power. She

Like Martha, we must hold on to what we know is true.

held on to what she knew was truth! Even though she'd seen Lazarus placed in the tomb with her own eyes, she believed totally that God would grant Jesus the power to raise him from the dead if He asked. From within her storm, Martha spoke the truth to which she was clinging: Even now, Jesus, you can bring Lazarus back to life! (John 11:22, implied).

APPLY As you review your Faith Focus card, what truth do you cling to, above the others, when the storm swirls around you?

_____

_____

_____

_____

Jesus replied to Martha's statement of faith with a spiritual truth. He was carefully guiding Martha from the truth she knew to the next step in her spiritual walk. He told Martha He was more than a man who receives power from God to raise the dead to life. *"I AM the resurrection and the life"* (John 11:25). With each response, Martha got closer to understanding the thunderous truth Jesus had just spoken.

Jesus was Martha's friend. He'd eaten at her table, fallen asleep on her couch, played with neighbor children in her front yard. She'd probably seen Him stub His toe and heard Him excuse Himself to go to the bathroom. In all ways, He was human to her. How difficult would it be for Martha's mind to make the leap from the certainty of the man she knew to the truth that He was God wearing flesh? Jesus was trying to show her that the Messiah, the Beloved Son of God, wasn't a separate entity from God—He was *Immanuel, —which means God with us* (Matthew 1:23).

In all ways, Jesus is Lord to us. In our mind's eye, we see Him seated at the right hand of the Father, receiving glory and honor and praise! My vision of Him is so fixed on the resurrected, ascended Christ that I confess I often lose sight of the humanness He shares with me. Do you sometimes have difficulty grasping He was a man who struggled with this world's problems and temptations just as you do, yet He remained sinless?

APPLY Has this study given you a new picture of Jesus as a Person who dealt with life in all its fullness? How has it increased your faith in Him as your Intercessor and your trust in Him as you face life's storms?

_____

_____

_____

_____

_____

_____

_____

With Jesus' words tumbling through her mind, Martha began her walk home. Jesus had asked her to send Mary to Him. Perhaps she was perplexed He didn't come home with her. Perhaps she was concerned Mary wouldn't agree to go to see Him. It wouldn't surprise her a bit. Jesus was probably the last person Mary wanted to see right now!

And then there was this phrase He'd said, with such a glow on His face: *"I am the resurrection and the life."* She'd never seen His eyes so intense. Her heart had pounded when He said it and she felt there was something very important in those words, just beyond her grasp. He'd often spoken to them of the resurrection of the dead at the last day when they'd all be with Him and with God forever, but what did He mean by saying HE was *"the resurrection and the life"?* What did it matter anyway? HE wasn't there when they needed Him to give life to Lazarus!

How I can identify with Martha! She'd been to Jesus and she came away feeling empty. She came away with words she didn't understand. She came away with words that didn't meet reality as she saw it. I remember going to God in a situation that was a devastating loss for me. He led me to Isaiah 29:5, 6, where I read these words: *"But your many enemies will become like fine dust, the ruthless hordes like blown chaff. Suddenly, in an instant, the LORD Almighty will come with thunder and earthquake and great noise, with windstorm and tempest and flames of a devouring fire."* I sat numbly, looking at these words, thinking, "Well, God, if You're planning to turn my enemies to dust and devour them in an instant, You're a little too late!" Those words made no sense to me. They didn't meet my present reality.

God didn't intervene in my situation and perform a miracle as He was planning to do in Mary and Martha's life. He might not intervene in your situation, either, although it's certainly possible; miracles still happen! But those words He gave me are truth. The day is coming when all the enemies of God's children will become as dust. Suddenly, in an instant, Jesus will appear, leading the hosts of heaven and there will be great thunder and earthquake and devouring fire. We must draw on the strength of believers around us when hard times come, and stand on the truth with them.

APPLY Has this study led you to Biblical truth that will prepare you to stand when God leaves you with words that don't match your reality? If so, how?

_____

_____

_____

_____

_____

_____

_____

_____

_____

_____

_____

"When the Jews who had been with Mary in the house, comforting her, noticed how quickly she got up and went out, they followed her, supposing she was going to the tomb to mourn there. When Mary reached the place where Jesus was and saw him, she fell at his feet and said, 'Lord, if you had been here, my brother would not have died.' When Jesus saw her weeping, and the Jews who had come along with her also weeping, he was deeply moved in spirit and troubled. 'Where have you laid him?' he asked. 'Come and see, Lord,' they replied. Jesus wept. Then the Jews said, 'See how he loved him!' But some of them said, 'Could not he who opened the eyes of the blind man have kept this man from dying?'" (John 11:31–37)

When Mary heard Jesus wanted to see her, she immediately left the house to go to Him. The people in the house followed her, assuming she was going to Lazarus's tomb. Imagine their surprise when she didn't turn the right direction! Can't you just hear the excited murmurs in the crowd when they figured out she was going to see Jesus? They probably expected Mary to be furious at Him because He didn't come when she asked Him to and they all wanted to be there to see what happened. Human nature hasn't changed, has it?

Mary was more distraught than Martha when she reached Jesus. Her first words were the same but her emotions were much different. Martha was able to move beyond the pain of Lazarus's death to express confidence in Jesus. Mary was so overwhelmed by sorrow, all she could do was fall at Jesus' feet and tell Him of her pain and disappointment. Jesus should've been there! Jesus should've done something! She'd heard Jesus say God would answer their prayers if they had faith. She had faith, she knew she did. Why did it all go so terribly wrong?

The two sisters responded to Jesus differently—and Jesus responded differently to them. He responded to Martha's calmness and confidence with a revelation of Himself beyond anything she'd ever seen or heard before. He responded to Mary's outpouring of emotion with compassion and emotion of His own. He didn't favor one sister over the other. He didn't scold one and praise the other. He simply responded to each one by blessing them where they were. How tender and loving Jesus is! He meets each of us where we are and gives us what we need.

As Jesus looked at Mary, weeping at His feet, and the crowd of friends and family also weeping, He became deeply troubled. He knew it was time to go to Lazarus's tomb and demonstrate the truth of the revelation He'd spoken to Martha. It was time to turn their sorrow into rejoicing. He knew the end of the story; He knew the final scene. Why, even with this knowledge, was He *"deeply moved in spirit and troubled"*?

Have you learned anything about Jesus over these weeks to explain why He would be so troubled when He saw Mary and her loved ones weeping? If so, what?

_____

_____

_____

_____

_____

Jesus meets each of us where we are and gives us what we need.

_____
_____
_____
_____

How tender our Savior's heart is toward His beloved! He grieved over Jerusalem and desired peace for her (Luke 19:41, 42). He shares with us the full range of human emotion: joy, disappointment, and grief. He desires to walk with us and to share our burdens. He is compassion, gentleness, and love. What a joy that our dear Savior longs to minister to us!

THE STORM PASSES: STAGGERING CHOICES

The Journey

DAY FOUR

"Jesus, once more deeply moved, came to the tomb. It was a cave with a stone laid across the entrance. 'Take away the stone,' he said. 'But, Lord,' said Martha, the sister of the dead man, 'by this time there is a bad odor, for he has been there four days.' Then Jesus said, 'Did I not tell you that if you believed, you would see if you believed, you would see the glory of God?' So they took away the stone. Then Jesus looked up and said, 'Father, I thank you that you have heard me. I knew that you always hear me, but I said this for the benefit of the people standing here, that they may believe that you sent me," When he had said this, Jesus called in a loud voice, "Lazarus, come out!" The dead man came out, his hands and feet wrapped with strips of linen, and a cloth around his face. Jesus said to them, 'Take off the grave clothes and let him go.' Therefore many of the Jews who had come to visit Mary, and had seen what Jesus did, put their faith in him. But some of them went to the Pharisees and told them what Jesus had done." (John 11:38–46)

When the group reached the tomb, I'm sure it was hard for everyone. Those of you who've lost a loved one know it's hard to go to the cemetery, especially at first. I've lost both my Mom and my father-in-law. When I go to one of the gravesites, there's always this initial shock—their names don't belong on that headstone! I don't want them to be there. Part of me loves and misses the physical body that's there. Yet, part of me feels no connection with the "tent" buried there because I believe everything that made them the people I love is now with God in Heaven. Does this odd, painful mix of feelings ever go away? Lazarus had only been in the tomb four days. It must have been very painful for Mary and Martha and their loved ones to go there.

In the midst of the pain, Jesus called out, asking for one more act of faith. As He stood before the tomb, He saw an obstacle in the way of the miracle He wanted to perform. *"Take away the stone," he said* (John 11:39a).

Was the stone really an obstacle to Jesus in the miracle He was about to perform? Why or why not?

_____
_____
_____

Was it an obstacle to Mary and Martha and the others gathered there? Why did Jesus ask for it to be rolled away?

_____

_____

_____

_____

We often have obstacles that must be rolled away before God can bless us.

Martha immediately objected to her Lord's request, didn't she? After all, it would be stinky and gross, and what would everyone think? Lazarus had already been dead four days, so what could be done, anyway? Remember, this is the same Martha who so confidently said, *"But I know that even now God will give you whatever you ask"* (John 11:22). Now it was time to put feet to those words, in front of everybody, and she wasn't quite so sure about it.

We often have obstacles to God's blessings, don't we? God whispers, "I'm ready to bless you but you need to allow Me to roll this away from your lifestyle, from your attitude, or from your emotions." Sometimes we stubbornly refuse and then we wonder why the blessings don't come. We wonder why we have to wait.

We might have a stone in our lives sealing a tomb full of bitterness or unforgiveness that must be opened and cleaned out before God can fully bless us. We may have a sealed tomb full of sin or sorrow from the past that God needs to redeem and fill with His light before He can bring an amazing resolution of our situation. Our obstacle might be fear or anger; we nurture it because we feel we deserve it. God knows this tomb has grasped control of our lives and He desires to clear it away, removing its stench so He can bring His power into our circumstances.

Many obstacles are too big to be handled alone. God is calling you to allow the believers around you to help you remove your obstacle. Mary and Martha couldn't remove the stone from the tomb on their own. They needed the strength of others around them. Certainly Jesus could've called Lazarus to walk right through the rock—what a sight that would have been! But He wanted Mary and Martha to complete an act of faith by having the stone rolled away.

APPLY As you look at the choices outlined in Chapter 6, what obstacles in your thoughts, emotions, or lifestyle prevent you from choosing to allow God to bless you? Do you need to ask God to lead you to loving, believing friends who can help you roll the obstacles away?

_____

_____

_____

_____

_____

_____

_____

How perfectly Habakkuk 1:5 fits into this story! The stone is rolled away. Mary and Martha, along with the rest of the crowd, are standing there, with no idea what Jesus could possibly have in mind. I can almost hear Jesus quote it: *"Look at* the opening of the tomb *and watch—and be utterly amazed. For I am going to do something in your circumstance that you would not believe, even if you were told"* (author's paraphrase).

I'm sure Jesus had everyone's attention. Can you hear the deafening silence as they held their breaths when Jesus spoke the words, "Lazarus, come out!"? And then . . . waves of shock, amazement, and pure joy swept through the crowd as Lazarus stumbled from the tomb.

Have you ever considered what Lazarus felt? Mary and Martha's miracle was his nightmare! One minute he was happily sitting before the throne of God, listening to angels sing. He was hanging with Abraham and Isaac and loved ones gone on before, having the time of his life. Then—bang! He was back on this miserable earth! He couldn't have been a happy camper. Now, I don't know if God let him experience four days of Heaven or not, since He knew Lazarus was going to return to Earth—that seems like cruel and unusual punishment to me. Perhaps all Lazarus was aware of was a split second, like deep slumber. All we know for sure is he found himself being unwrapped by two ecstatic sisters, and he was very possibly confused about what had happened.

God's purpose for this storm wasn't done, even as Mary and Martha were celebrating Lazarus's resurrection. Many of the Jews who'd come to mourn Lazarus's death had now seen Jesus raise him to life and, because of this, they placed their faith in Him as the Christ. Others went to the Pharisees and described what had happened. News of this miracle was the last straw that led the Sanhedrin and the high priest, Caiaphas, to issue orders for Jesus' arrest (John 11:46-57). God used this storm in the life of this small family from Bethany to impact the eternal life of many people and to set in motion the single most important event to ever occur since the creation of the world: the crucifixion of Jesus Christ, making salvation available for all mankind. Truly, we may never know all the purposes God is working out through the storms He allows to enter our lives.

> *We may never know all the purposes God is working out through the storms He allows to enter our lives.*

The Journey

DAY FIVE

LESSONS MADE REAL

In this last day of our journey together, I ask that you look back over your path of valleys and mountaintops. Is there a difficult time that stands out in your memory? Come with me as we apply God's truth to our individual lives.

A Dark Horizon: Medical Emergency
Several years ago, my best friend died and I hurried to the airport—at least I've been told I hurried to the airport. As I waited for the shuttle to pick me up and take me to the terminal, I collapsed on the ground and had a seizure. For those of you who are familiar with seizures, memory is drastically affected. I don't remember the events from an hour before or for two days after.

I'd never had a seizure before and, in that moment, my life was forever changed. The dark clouds approached and I had no idea how this would impact my future.

I'm sure each of you has found herself facing a crisis. Was it a health problem, as mine was? Was it a financial issue or difficulty with a relationship? Look back over your life and choose a tough situation you faced and describe it briefly:

_____

_____

_____

_____

_____

It's such a strange feeling to have people tell you about the events of several days when you have no memory of them at all. Evidently, I spent several hours in the emergency room while the doctors determined exactly what had happened. My husband, Charles, arrived, a little unnerved by the whole thing. I was convinced the doctors were all wrong and that this was a mistake. After all, I had a very busy life and I didn't have time to deal with any of this.

How well I remember my insistence that nothing was wrong with me during an appointment with the neurologist! The whole thing was just a hiccup in my plans and I wasn't going to let it affect me. I spent many hours telling God He could just fix it because I didn't want to mess with it. I was convinced He would disperse the clouds before they could interfere with my plans.

How did you respond to the storm you saw bearing down on you? Did you go into stubborn denial, or respond with panic? How did you pray during this time?

_____

_____

_____

_____

_____

_____

The Storm Strikes: Facing the Changes

Over the next few weeks, my life was a shambles. I wouldn't be allowed to drive for six months! But that was ridiculous—how was I supposed to meet the kids' schedule, do the shopping, and continue to work on my college degree? The list of responsibilities went on and on.

Where was God? What was His problem? Couldn't He see that this just wasn't going to work? I was angry and confused. As the doctor explained the changes that would invade my life, I became even more angry and depressed. I searched God's Word for promises this would all go away and that I'd be fine.

More seizures followed as we struggled to find a medication that would control them. The first one didn't work; I was allergic to the next one. I went through my days in fear another seizure would strike at any moment. The spells of memory loss were so frustrating. We finally found a medication that controlled the problem but had one "serious" side effect: It caused weight gain! You can imagine how I reacted to that. I'd finally got rid of the extra weight from my pregnancy and now I was going to be bursting out of my clothes again.

My life was no longer my own. I prayed and prayed but God remained silent. How did your particular situation impact your life as the storm moved in and took over?

_____

_____

_____

_____

_____

_____

_____

Stepping through the Storm

Every time I had a doctor's appointment, I was sure he'd tell me I was healed. After all, I claimed every healing verse I could find. I read God's Word out loud to Him, demanding He obey it. He's the Lord who heals (Psalm 103:3 Jeremiah 17:14). I focused on the accounts in Scripture that described His healing work. So, why wasn't He doing anything?

I was so angry, I stopped talking to God, except to yell at Him. I lost all faith that He could resolve this situation. I refused to see He had a plan. It all seemed hopeless. I had to depend on friends and family to take me and my kids where we needed to go. I canceled many of my activities. I found myself sitting at home, pouting.

Did I use this season of solitude to draw closer to Him? Did I spend time in prayer and in His Word? No, I just complained. But even in my stubbornness, God reached out to me. He led me to 2 Corinthians 12:7–9. In this passage, Paul talks about a "thorn in his flesh." Three times he asked God to heal him and three times God refused. Why? The answer is found in verse 9: *"But he said to me, 'My grace is sufficient for you, for my power is made perfect in weakness.'"*

I realized God wasn't going to remove my "thorn in the flesh." Was He sufficient when the memory loss came? Was He sufficient when I needed transportation and no one was available? I looked at my circumstances, and my needs seemed overwhelming. How could His power make it all "perfect"?

I needed an attitude change. I needed to lift my eyes off the hopelessness of my situation and onto the hope God gives us. I needed to allow trust to replace panic and peace to replace desperation. The One who controlled the universe could certainly find me a ride to the grocery store!

The promises of God's presence and love are true, even in difficult circumstances.

Rather than complain, I should have praised Him and been thankful my first seizure occurred when I was standing in a parking lot, not when I was driving. Had that happened, I could've been seriously hurt along with pedestrians and/or those in the cars around me. As the weeks passed by, I should have praised Him that the medication was working and that no more seizures occurred. I should have praised Him for the many friends who prayed for me and were willing to drive me, even when it was inconvenient for them.

Slowly God brought me to an increased faith in Him. He was in control. He did have a plan. He was taking care of me. The promises of His presence and love were true, even in difficult circumstances.

When the storm in your life raged on and you realized God was going to take you through it rather than remove you from it, how did you respond? How did He bring you to a point of praise, thanksgiving, and dependence on Him? How did His promises give you peace and assurance?

_____

_____

_____

_____

_____

Choices to Make

I tried to return to normal, but there were lingering effects of the seizure disorder not resolved by the medication. I struggled with my memory; often, in midsentence, I forgot what I was saying. Sometimes a word came flying out of my mouth and it bore no resemblance to the word I wanted to say. My thoughts wandered aimlessly. People wondered if I'd gone crazy—and so did I.

Day-to-day activities were a challenge because I was easily distracted. I walked into a room and forgot what I came for. I left a smattering of uncompleted chores behind me and I could never find my keys. Trying to run errands without a detailed list of where I needed to go and what I needed to do was a disaster. Satan taunted me and told me I'd never get any better.

It was tempting to hide but I'm too stubborn for that. I chose to call upon God's power to fight and to conquer my weaknesses. I prayed continually and asked Him to teach me ways to compensate. I kept a notepad with me and wrote down chores or grocery items as they came to mind. I spoke more slowly to allow my thoughts to keep up with my words. I used the memories of others—"Remind me to . . ." became a cherished phrase.

I had to redefine my world and come to peace with it. I could choose to be frustrated or to trust God's provision. I could choose to be angry or to rest in His peace. I could choose to remain fiercely independent or to learn to lean on God. I could choose to be defeated or to learn new habits that overcame my struggles. God's steadfast presence gave me the strength to choose victory.

None of these choices came easy and most of them have to be made day after day. I'm no longer embarrassed when my words stumble; I just laugh and give it another try. I'm no longer so frustrated when I lose something or forget what I'm supposed to be doing; I retrace my steps until something sparks my memory.

Although these problems have become a part of my life, the tricks I use to compensate for them have as well. I've learned to be content with the life God planned for me and to rely on Him every day. God was and is sufficient to meet my needs.

What choices have you made to find peace with the effects left behind by your specific situation? What choices do you still need to make? How have you found God to be sufficient for your needs?

_____

_____

_____

_____

_____

_____

_____

Claim the Fruit of the Journey
Precious ladies, I'm so proud of you! This has been a difficult journey but you have stayed the course; you've made it. You are standing tall and strong in your heart (even if you feel as if your body's fallen flat on its face). Listen to the words of God as He praises you for your journey:

> *"Today I have made you a fortified city, an iron pillar and a bronze wall to stand against the whole land."* (Jeremiah 1:18a)

> *"You will keep in perfect peace him whose mind is steadfast, because he trusts in you."* (Isaiah 26:3)

> *"And the God of all grace, who called you to his eternal glory in Christ, after you have suffered a little while, will himself restore you and make you strong, firm and steadfast."* (1 Peter 5:10)

> *"If we endure, we will also reign with him."* (2 Timothy 2:12)

Writing these pages, praying for you as each chapter was completed, has been a journey for me as well. There's been indescribable joy, realizing God might *"comfort those in any trouble with the comfort I myself have received from God"* (2 Corinthians 1:4, author's paraphrase). There were also moments of emotion as God led me to deal with unfinished business from my own past experiences. Through it all, my prayer has been and is for you to see God, in all His love and compassion; for it to be His voice alone you hear.

It is my prayer that these weeks have confirmed in your heart the love your Father has for you, a love far beyond your understanding. Your life is a journey, lovingly planned by your Father, and He desires more than anything to walk it with you. Each circumstance, good and bad, is weighed in His heart against His purposes for your earthly life and your eternal life.

Your life is a journey, lovingly planned by your Father, and He desires more than anything to walk it with you.

Each event is designed to bear fruit in your life: joy in His presence, trust in His provision, peace in His loving care, and so much more the world cannot steal away.

His vision of your life is always toward your completeness—toward the person you will be when you stand before Him and He welcomes you into your eternal home. His perspective is eternal; His work-bench is earthly. Trust Him and surrender to the work of His loving hands.

As you journey through this life, sisters, encourage one another. Walk beside each other, in laughter and in tears. Comfort each other when the thunder rolls; rejoice together when the sun shines. Trials may come, but look to the day when this earthly life will fade and we will celebrate together at the marriage feast of the Lamb.

Works Cited

1. Jay P. Green, Sr., ed. *The Interlinear Bible, Hebrew-Greek-English, Second Edition* (Peabody, MA: Hendrickson Publishers, 1986), 934.

2. Spiros Zodhiates, ed. *The Complete Word Study Dictionary: New Testament* (Chattanooga, TN: AMG Publishers, 1993), #1679.

3. Walter C. Kaiser, Jr., *Expositor's Bible Commentary, Vol. 2, Exodus,* ed. Frank E. Gæbelin (Grand Rapids Michigan: Zondervon, 1990), 553-559.

4. Ibid., 587-591.

5. Leon Morris, *NICNT, the Gospel According to John* (Grand Rapids Michigan: William B. Eerdmans Publishing Co., 1995), 157.

6. Green, Sr., ed., *Interlinear Bible*, 739.

7. Zodhiates, ed., *The Complete Word Study Dictionary: New Testament,* #1487:IB, 505.

8. Ronald F. Youngblood, Herbert Lockyer, Sr., eds., *Nelson's New Illustrated Bible Dictionary* (Nashville, TN: Thomas Nelson Publishers, 1995), 1164-1165.

9. Howard F. Voss, *Nelson's New Illustrated Bible Manners and Customs* (Nashville, TN: Thomas Nelson Publishers, 1999), 462–464.

10. Warren Baker, D.R.E., Eugene Carpenter, Ph.D., *The Complete Word Study Dictionary: Old Testament* (Chattanooga, TN: AMG Publishers, 2003), #1368.

11. Zodhiates, *The Complete Word Study Dictionary: New Testament.* #5432.

12. Ibid., #842.

13. Baker, Carpenter, Eds., *The Complete Word Study Dictionary: Old Testament*, #4284.

14. Ibid., #7965

15. Ibid., #7451.

16. Ibid., #8615II

17. Ibid., #319

Notes